*Cover artwork inspired by*
*Harry and the Hendersons, by author.*

# TELUKE A BIG FOOT ACCOUNT

## A Personal Account of Interaction with an Older Race of Spiritual Beings

by

### WHITE SONG EAGLE

authorHOUSE®

AuthorHouse™
1663 Liberty Drive, Suite 200
Bloomington, IN 47403
www.authorhouse.com
Phone: 1-800-839-8640

First published by AuthorHouse 11/19/2008

ISBN: 978-1-4389-1306-3 (sc)

Library of Congress Control Number: 2008909113

Printed in the United States of America
Bloomington, Indiana

This book is printed on acid-free paper.

All of the artwork presented is by the author

# *Dedication*

I dedicate this to the breath of life, in awe.

I give to You my attention and devotion in Oneness as

Consciousness. AHO!

WHITE SONG EAGLE

# Contents

# *Foreward*

AT FIRST GLANCE, ONE MIGHT ask, "Why would someone who had the experience of being abducted by extraterrestrials be asked to write the forward for a book that is basically about an essentially life-long Bigfoot encounter?" I asked myself that same question when White Song came to me and asked me to write this for her. I just didn't think I could do her or her book justice since I had never had her particular kind of encounter. What I didn't realize at the time was that we had, indeed, shared something in common, despite the differences in out encounters.

When anyone experiences **any** type of paranormal phenomena, they can pretty much count on the fact that they are going to be in for a hard time if they try to tell anyone about what they have been through.

I'm not talking about good old fashioned, healthy skepticism. I like to think of myself as a skeptic. I always exhaust all prosaic explanations before I begin to look in the more "exotic" direction. I have questioned parts of my own story time and time again, trying to believe that there must be some rational explanation for things I have seen in my own life. And I know that White Song has tried to do the same.

I learned a long time ago that there is more to this life than meets the eye, more than we may **ever** come to understand. And I've also learned that there are some folks out there who will **never** be convinced of anything that won't fit neatly into their own little world—no matter how much evidence one can produce.

All I have ever asked of anyone was for them to listen to me. I never expected anyone to believe me. I told them what I knew to be factual and left the theorizing up to the individual, allowing each to find their own "common zone".

White Song tells us her story as only she can, with the hope that as we read, as her life unfolds before our eyes, we will listen with an open mind and an open heart. Not just for her, but also for all the rest of life that teems just beyond our grasp. Simply because we can't see, feel, hear or touch something, that doesn't mean it can't be real or that it can't exist. That may be one of life's hardest lessons and the one that will do us all the most good to learn.

Debbie Jordan-Kauble
(Author: <u>ABDUCTED: The Intruders Story Continues</u>)
Kokomo, Indiana
June, 1995

# *Introduction*

ALL OF MY LIFE I have been moving in and out of a state of hyper-awareness that has allowed me to interact with unusual beings of a non-ordinary reality. Our everyday world is something we all take quite for granted. We buy into conceptual reality first as disembodied entities through mass agreement before we enter this plane and second when we accept what we are taught things are, what is "real" and what is not "real."

Conventional reality is a mass agreement of concepts, a world held together by a fabric of beliefs. Take a good look at cultural differences and it becomes evident that we live in a world of "stories" or, our opinions of what and how things are...

To the dominant society a dream is merely a fantasy of make believe. To many indigenous people the dream world is a separate reality that they enter, participate in, such as heal or steal, and can bring material evidence back with them. This loose hold on conceptual reality also affords other cultures such freedom as shape-shifting, duality and even time travel.

To speak of non-ordinary reality with those who believe in conventional reality, is often a threat to the very fabric of their world and causes a myriad of reactions from being called a liar and having "great imagination" to anger and outrage. It affronts the finite body, inhabited by an infinite being, because it is a contradiction to itself.

I have never fully bought into this system of conceptual reality. The beings my sister and I interacted with were as real as ourselves. I continued to interact with them rather than being dissuaded by others that they were not real. We brought back evidence with us as we reentered a locked house and left wet grass in our beds. Loosen the concepts and you loosen the fabric of this world. It enabled Jesus.

This hyper-awareness is a "Second Attention" that we all have. Yours can be tapped into and awakened by anyone else who is using this Second Attention. However, it remains up to the individual whether or not he will allow conscious knowledge of the information coming through.

So when I tell people I have taken care of a family of Sasquatch it often causes them to feel threatened. And then to tell them that I, in return, have been taken care of and watched over by the Star People (whom some of my people refer to as ancestors) ever since I was two or three years old, well, who's likely to believe me?

Since both of these unusual beings walk in a parallel world, I cannot speak of one without bringing the other along. UFO abductees are presently crawling out of the woodwork. One prominent note reported often by the abductees is that the encounter has been erased from their minds. They often report being told by the aliens that they have to forget or they will die.

I believe that part of what is meant by this is that our psyche is so fragile we ourselves will not translate the incident from the Second Attention into waking consciousness without great trauma, unless we are ready. We must wait for time to pass until we are capable, on some deeper level, of dealing with our fears of the unknown in conjunction with our own portrayal of reality. In this book the reader will begin to understand how this is done.

This Second Attention is apart from regular consciousness unless merged by will, which is located in the solar plexus or energy storehouses located on the front of the body.

What goes on in the parallel world and is viewed by the Second Attention will remain outside normal awareness until we allow it to be translated for our understanding.

It is something like two separate lenses acting independently of each other unless joined purposely from one focal point. You might even compare it to the headlights of an automobile, where the dim lights representing our regular consciousness that we use all the time, and the bright beams equal the Second Attention.

When the bright beams are triggered, they see everything the dim lights see, plus a lot more. Meanwhile, the dims are still on simultaneously, but can only 'see' what the dim lights themselves shine on. Then later, when the bright lights are shut off, the dims may not even be aware they were part of the greater perception. They just continue functioning (perceiving) at their usual level.

If they were joined to one focal point (by will) it would be equal to having the driver's perception included, able to see what both beams are 'looking at'. It is up to the dim lights if it should know what the bright lights are seeing. Most people don't want to know.

Even though some abductees may fight and insist they will remember and that they want to, the physical fear factor, or body consciousness aborts its memory anyway.

I might also add that this is not to say that the ET.s do not assist in this process, possibly by helping to close this door (possibly a chakra, or energy center, of the body). As children, we are trained to short-circuit the main focal point where both worlds can be viewed. This maintains a mass agreement of what people choose to believe is reality.

Occasionally it happens that we are awakened momentarily to full consciousness and are surprised then to view two separate incidents going on. Conversations and interactions take place that we might not be able to remember later. What accounts for this memory loss? When someone has an encounter with that other reality, or the beings that exist within it, they can become traumatized. When a person is traumatized, they simply swallow a larger piece of information than is comfortable. It takes time to digest and properly assimilate this new reality. But even when this happens, they remain within their own safety limits, because their will acts like a safety valve. It is their own will that allows an alternate reality to become cognizant in their conscious mind.

I am recording a year in my life during approximately the spring of 1973 to the summer of 1974, during which I interacted with and began investigating my UFO case with Norma Crota of Mutual UFO Network ("MUFON").

It was also discovered that Debbie Jordan Kauble, the subject that the book INTRUDERS was written about, lived just the next town over during the same time my present story was unfolding. She is the author of the book ABDUCTED: The Intruders Story Continues and kindly wrote the forward to this book.

While scientific methods have a legitimate place in research, they fail to produce consequential proof of things beyond physical reality [corporality]. At these times, it becomes necessary for the sake of the enhancement of knowledge to incorporate what Dr. James R. Butler, a Zoologist in Alberta, Canada, terms a "Higher Sensory Perception," or HSP. All creatures are endowed with it. After all, are we not to believe the dogs, horses, cattle, cats and birds, who (even if locked up) become highly agitated in the presence of unseen entities? Man too, is an animal endowed with this gift, if we would but only use our "whiskers."

Among the "professional" researchers, there is a general consensus that a long trail of credentials is a prerequisite for any credibility. They dismiss empirical evidence that does not conform to their own (often biased) beliefs, that Sasquatch can only be a finite animal, if indeed it exists at all. I have no intention of convincing them or anyone else that there is more to reality than that. Quantum science and quantum mechanics does that for me.

Having done "a five month field study in the Jane Goodall tradition," social scientist and anthropologist Jack Lapseritis is one exception in the Big Foot research field. Although having little interest in the paranormal, he returned convinced of, as his book title explains, "The Psychic Sasquatch: A UFO Connection!" Over the years he has been rewarded with numerous first-hand encounters with Big Foot as well as meeting other folks with experiences such as mine. There is growing evidence of these paranormal events, taken from many statements of people who have encountered Sasquatch, which substantiate much of the happenings of this book.

Although this story is unique in content, it is not as unusual as one might first believe. The Big Foot reports one hears about from the media are generally from people with little experience with this non-ordinary reality. They tend to file reports of such occurrences that are viewed from fear or lack of understanding. Often these reporters appear to be intimidated by the unknown.

Yet I have found that there are also people besides myself who are not afraid of the unknown. The beings who protect the Sasquatch seek out people with open minds to assist. There are many people doing just that. You don't hear about it because one cannot advertise such activity and maintain the privacy needed. It is counter-productive to the activity.

I would like to explain that I have learned to call the female Star Person who worked with me on the "ship" all my life - the one who whisked me away into the night - by the name Zanna. As she began guiding me on the Second Attention early in my life, it at first puzzled me who this was that was speaking to me in my head - down here, in my every-day world. She directed my attention into the heavens, reflecting in my mind the memory of her on the "ship" last night, so I would know who was assisting me.

When I would listen to her, she would carefully guide me away from trouble and back to safety. Thus, it was she that guided me to interact with the Sasquatch.

During all of my interactions with the Sasquatch, except for brief glimpses in the final good-bye scene and when he astral projected into the house at the very beginning, the Sasquatch were in their invisible form. They do have the ability to leave their bodies and travel about in spirit from place to place, but this is not what I mean when I speak of their invisibility.

In this dematerialized state, they are physically in another dimension. They remain completely unseen by the eye, yet they can retain weight and mass, and can be felt with the hands as well as be felt when they touch you.

When they astral project, they can be noticed with the peripheral vision of the eyes, whereas in this other dimension, they cannot, except for occasional glimpses of the red eyes or a body part showing through. Only through psychic ability in connecting the Second Attention to the waking consciousness, can they be seen at those times, that is, when they are in the other dimension.

Let me emphasize that all conversations with them were telepathic. But I would like to elaborate a little on what telepathy actually is. Telepathy is the transference of information, knowledge from one person to another and it doesn't have to be words. It is not necessarily a conscious thing. In fact, being directed by our higher self, we often have no control over it.

For instance, have you ever lain awake at night with what seems like a running conversation going on in your head, which you cannot shut off? You may or may not even know who it is being directed to or from (depending on whether you are sending or receiving). This is often telepathy. Your higher self is in contact with someone and an exchange of information is transpiring. It can be quite difficult to shut off or shut out, because it is your central core **Being** that ultimately has control.

Most people are not aware of how many thoughts go through their minds that are not their own. But then again, how many readers can recall even a half hour of their own silent thoughts while traveling to or from work today? The thoughts of others often influence your day.

Included in the transference of information in telepathy are the sensory channels of sight and feelings as well. The Sasquatch, Zanna and I often shared each other's eyes. If one of us could not see something for themselves, the other would look at it for them and relay the information. We also shared physical sensation this way, as well. When he experienced something new, I also re-experienced the newness of it just as he felt it, even though it was not "new" to my own senses.

These wonderful qualities are a part or the reason Sasquatch are successful in evading the Bigfoot hunter. Author/researcher Jack Lapseritis explains in his book that Sasquatch will use hawks and crows as sentinels at times. They simply use a bird's eye view of a situation they do not wish to get close to. I have shared this experience first hand! Quite a good reason so few Big Foot are encountered.

I found these telepathic interactions a joyous blessing to be exposed to. It created a bond among the three of us (the male and female Sasquatch, and me) that secures a person in a way that is difficult to experience in modern Western society. Something our ignorant society sorely lacks.

Some adjustments have been made in the documentation of this account. I cannot be certain that everything is in the exact order in which it occurred, though I have taken great pains to be as accurate as possible.

Also, their communication is so basic it was difficult for me to regress to his limited vocabulary during the year of our interaction. I would almost say they don't have a language, but knowledge. They just understood what some things are.

Therefore, it is nearly impossible after fifteen years for me to recall the exact words he used. It seemed wiser to paraphrase his thoughts and say precisely what I understood him to mean.

For instance, he would include me by saying "You People", when he meant "Your People." I got him to use a few of our words, which he did reluctantly. I asked him to use the word "your" so he and I could relate better.

They are such simple people it was as beautiful as it was confusing to relate to them. They are so uncomplicated that in their world most things have no name at all. They know what things do and how they are affected by them and that was good enough. Food is food, but this family did not distinguish types of food. The thing in the sky (the sun) was a good something, and insects were things they brushed off their food before eating.

It should be noted that each individual Sasquatch is as unique a person as you and I, being made up from a conglomerate of personal experiences and environmental exposure as we ourselves are. Just as no single profile fits each of us, so it is with Sasquatch. Keep in mind that these are my own experiences and though they are not my only encounters with Sasquatch, they are true, yet incomplete, because of the variables involved.

With this particular family, it was confusing for me to revert my vocabulary to their level and bridge the gap of their simplicity. I made innumerable mistakes in the relationship because of this. Likewise, all the words and idioms I used confused Teluke and broadened his distrust of me.

In my associations with Teluke, he often tried to bully me and threatened to kill me. But I know they prefer to intimidate rather than resort to violence. Otherwise, they would not have allowed us to take over all the green spaces.

I guess because of some natural innocence in me, I trusted in the goodness I saw in him. I believed that as long as I didn't threaten him he would have no reason to follow through with his threats. So, I rarely received more than a snarling reprimand.

Common sense and respect is a key factor here. He, like most, was 99% bluff, but I weathered some pretty rough gales to discover this. Any fool can get themselves killed, though Sasquatch are not killers. They are reasonable people and they simply want us to be reasonable also.

Teluke loved children and babies of any kind. He showed a feminine kind of gentleness and empathy towards them that was heart warming to see. Sasquatch appreciate the innocence of children. I guess it's because they share that innocence.

As our time together progressed, Teluke used our words more and he also understood more of them. He more easily adjusted to our language than I did to his irrelevant need of one!

The Star People have been instrumental in all of my interactions with the Sasquatch. Because of my consensual 'employment' to assist, they have kept tabs on my health and welfare. If there were any changes in my vibrations, usually surfacing in my 'light' which they monitored, they were interested and/or concerned and made the appropriate changes. So it was on one occasion when they came to get me for a "check-up."

"What is going on in your life? Your light has changed!" Zanna, who was always in charge of me on the ship, said with concern in her eyes. They always communicated telepathically with me, rather than using their verbal language, which was a series of clicks and clacks like a porpoise.

"I have gotten married! Can I bring him to meet you? He's really wonderful!" I asked her. The regard Zanna had for me was so overpowering that it felt like these beings had a direct conduit to God, flowing The Creator's love directly outward. They in no way adulterated it, as compared to the dim watered-down version which we mundane humans must share among ourselves. I felt very comforted in their presence.

"Yes, we <u>will</u> meet him," she affirmed.

Later, my new husband and I were whisked away up into the ship as we traveled down a dark road at night. Not being used to this, Byron, my husband, was terribly frightened.

Please understand that he was no sissy. He was a gentle and kind soul, but hearty and a good wrestler. I have seen much bigger men back down when faced with the bizarre happenings of this non-ordinary reality. In fact, I would say those who must grab up weapons to shoot the unknown are dealing with even more terror.

So, it is no shame to him that he reacted in what must be termed a normal fear.

It is pretty well documented that if you are going to fight, you lose your mobility with the ET's. They 'paralyze' you and take full control of you. That is how it was with Byron. They floated him about, while he was emotionally kicking and screaming. I, on the other hand, have experienced this all my life and usually look forward to it. I am not often afraid (though in all honesty there is at times an underlying dread,) therefore they allow me to remain in my own control for the most part. My husband was out of his mind with terror, screaming continually.

I asked Zanna, in the brilliant interior of the ship, if there was anything I could do to help.

She said, "Yes, try to calm him down and help get him in position."

I walked up behind the little gray beings standing before Byron and parting them aside, tried to get his attention onto me.

I began screaming at him in an even louder volume than he, so he could hear me, and put my face right in his, inches close, nose to nose. "It's okay! I am here! It's okay! I love you! I am here! I am here! It's okay!"

Eventually, he saw me and began to hear me. His volume dropped a bit with his lessening fear. As he calmed down some, I took his arms, which were frozen in front of his chest, and lowered them to his sides, where an electrical or magnetic field secured them again.

This set him off once more, and he began screaming, "What are you doing? Now I can't move at all! Why are you able to move around? You act like you're helping them! You act like you know them!" he said accusingly.

Seeing a completely different side of the whole thing for the first time, it didn't occur to me to do anything else but tell the truth.

"Well, I am. I do! This is my family!" I said, expecting him to accept them as he had me. But, he went into hysterical shock, from which he would never completely recover.

"What? You said those other people were your family! You never told me this! You deceived me! You should have told me this!" At this point, he totally lost control and screamed in terror for the rest of the event.

When we were finally returned to our home, I checked the house for intruders, looking behind every door, sofa, table and closet.

"What are you doing?" he asked me.

"Just checking," I said.

"That's a good idea," he agreed.

Both of us were already beginning to forget consciously why and what had just transpired.

The next morning we found we had both had the same "dream." Something about my having hand cuffed him. He was extremely moody and I knew I was on thin ice, so I gave him plenty of elbow room.

By noon, he had gotten over the dream, and I assumed things were back to normal. However, over the following three years, Zanna expected me to continue my work in assisting the Sasquatch. But each incident pretty much fell apart because of Byron's inability to deal with the reality of it. Even though he did try, he couldn't deal with his fear.

The last alternative to continue my work was for Zanna to plant the suggestion in him, to move from our own little rented house into his folk's house, on their farm, so the Star People could bring to me a needed situation for my work/ my spiritual growth. And so the story begins.

I tell you now with my integrity before me, that all of these accounts are true. If you find this unacceptable that is fine, then read it as entertaining food for thought. Your exposure to it is enough.

The names of the people in the story have been changed to protect the identity of the individuals involved. Those people who truly know me, know me to be honest and credible and true to my word, even if much of my life happens to be incredible. To those who have stood by me at times when I doubted my own sanity, I am eternally grateful and I am not afraid anymore to be doubted by others. It doesn't change the truth.

Respectfully,
I am
White Song Eagle

The excerpts preceding each chapter
are taken from the book

ELEVATIONS,
or AGLA ON Dawning

By White Song Eagle

# CHAPTER ONE

## *New Neighbors*

*…Oh Zanna, Oh Zanna*

*Oh Zanna in the highest!…*

"YOU ARE BEING GIVEN A Sasquatch family to take care of." The words drifted softly through the open window of my mind like sunlight on a gossamer curtain, breathing gently in the morning breeze. It seemed like an ordinary day to me, but I was giddy inside. It was just plain good to have sunshine! I was anxious to get outside!

"She is having her baby today." Zanna spoke seemingly over my shoulder. My body ignored the words themselves, but had its reaction of excitement. I felt like it was my own birthday! My mind was way off in its own world though, where I continued the conversation.

"Can I go help her? I'm good with the horses and mid-wifing other babies!"

I had always loved babies, but even more so since I had been able to participate in several births. The horses were due to birth soon, and I was anxiously waiting to bring the new life into the world.

"You had better wait. Teluke can get pretty nasty. He will want to protect his family. You could upset Teleel while she is vulnerable. It is better if you wait." Zanna was pleased with my anticipation, but also concerned for my safety.

"Do you think he would hurt me?" I asked. It hadn't occurred to me that I would receive any reception other than happy.

"He could try to kill you, if you interfered right now. Your chances are better after the baby is born", said Zanna.

'Chances? Kill me? Hey, I don't want to do this at all if he is that kind of mean!' I thought, as I momentarily caught a glimpse of the depth of this.

"We will do what we can. We will be watching. You will have to do battle with him anyway, soon," Zanna said.

What? What was she talking about? "I wouldn't stand a chance! He's a man, plus he's super human! I don't want to fight anybody! I love them!" I said incredulously.

I was scared to the bone at the thought of this ridiculous notion and put the idea out of my mind.

"Will you tell me when the baby is born and when it is safe?" I asked. Zanna's smile in her voice assured me she would.

I went outside and sat on the back steps. I didn't know what to do to pass the morning so I poked finger holes into the damp, soft soil and then got a stick and began to thumb off the bark.

The morning passed, but the minutes magnified into hours. By early afternoon, I felt as though two days had passed before Zanna spoke to me again, somewhere in the back part of my mind.

"She's had her baby. You may go visit them now, if you wish," she said.

My mind raced. "Will you be with me in case he tries to kill me?" I asked.

"Yes," Zanna reassured me, "but I don't think he will."

In every-day reality I knew something was different and told my mother-in-law (Mom) that I just felt "so good" today, as though it were my birthday or something!

She laughed, and was happy to see excitement in my eyes and suggested getting a cake at the store this coming Friday. I told her I was going to explore the woods out back and went outside. I had never been in those woods. It belonged to a man who lived behind it. The wooded lot was a small, two or three acre plot that ran adjacent to the back of our five acre horse farm's pasture.

Casually, I strolled down the lane to the woods. The sun was warm, the air fresh and balmy on this perfect day. The only thing missing were the bird's songs which normally filled the woods. The birds had vacated the wood approximately one week before.

I entered the woods from the side, stepping softly to avoid snapping sticks and disturbing the expected wildlife. I also entered into a state of hyper-awareness where I was vividly cognizant of the real facts involved, yet leaving the placid physical body ignorant of much of the incident.

As I picked my way carefully through the plant life and sticks, I was shocked to realize I had walked right up on, what to my conscious mind was a bear, sound asleep next to a log. I gasped at the shock of my predicament, as there are no bears in Indiana. But, yet, here I was, apparently at the foot of one, which I would undoubtedly surprise.

Sure enough, my gasp startled it, and it bolted from its nest. To my amazement, as well as my relief, it disappeared immediately, yanking a young one up off the ground, which also then disappeared. I heard the Mother apologize and coo to the startled baby.

I was truly relieved to see it gone when I heard at the same instant, an unknown bird whistle a single note. I had but just an instant to wonder what kind of bird it was, when my "Second Attention" was awakened by a horrendous snarling sound. Something was charging at me from my left.

"What did you do to my mate?" a male voice exploded within my mind with its menace. I felt I was about to be devoured alive, as he rushed at me! I had a brief and strange impression that I was an infiltrator, and unless I identified myself immediately, I would be killed!

"It's me! It's me," I cried out. I had expected them to know all about me from Zanna, because I knew all about them.

"I didn't do anything! I'm sorry! I won't hurt you! I didn't mean to bother you!" I felt it was pertinent that I explain as much as I could, as quickly as possible.

He backed off but his tone was still plenty serious. "What are you doing here?" he demanded in a voice that one does not ignore.

"I came in here for healing. I need the woods and trees and birds to heal me. I won't bother you. I love you. I won't stay long," I said quickly.

My ignorant vessel seemed dazed as I gazed around, taking notice of the plant life that was eaten, as well as worn down in the trampled living space. Beside the nest from which I had disturbed the female, lay, what at first I had thought to be a partly eaten animal or entrails. Closer inspection revealed it to be a placenta. My conscious mind was wondering what animal had given birth, as it was too large for a fox or canine, too small for a horse, and there were really no deer to be seen in rural New Palestine, then.

"It's mine. I just had a baby," came the sweetest feminine voice into my mind. I realized that the placenta was so fresh that the flies hadn't found it yet, so I suggested they bury it so they wouldn't be discovered. They both acknowledged that they hadn't had time to do that yet.

"May I see your baby?" I asked, expecting her, as any new mother, to proudly show-off her child, but instead she cowered and blinked herself out of even my Second Attention. Her actions were answer enough.

"You must leave," the huge male told me. Having apparently assessed me a bit, his tone was more relaxed, but firm.

I seemed to be receiving all this information on several levels.

1. The First Attention or regular consciousness was all but completely ignorant of anything more than a forceful presence. 2. Second Attention could see something of which I didn't care to try to figure out, and 3. Part of me knew these beings on a personal basis and well knew they were human beings, these people we know as Sasquatch. This last portion of my consciousness saw both realities.

"I came here to heal. I won't bother you and I don't plan to stay long. I love you. I won't hurt you. Just ignore me and go on about your business." I spoke reassuringly as I placed my carcass on a log, in what must have been their living space, by the looks of things.

He was still assessing me, but seemed to be somewhat accepting, yet cautious of this strange intruder.

"Do you have any guns?" he asked me.

"No! I don't believe in guns or killing things," I replied.

As though with a second thought, he came back with "Do you have any knives or other weapons?"

"I thought for a moment then said "I have a knife at home, but I don't use it for hurting things. Why? Do you need one? I could get it for you!"

"No! We don't need those things like you people. Our way is better," he responded.

The animosity in his voice made his view of our world rather obvious. I asked why he had asked about weapons.

"You people think we are animals. You shoot at us!" he responded.

I assured him that I knew they were not animals and that I had only love for them. Every once in a while, glancing toward the female Teleel, I could get a glimpse of the fuzzy babe in her arms upon which she would go further into wherever they disappear to, to the point where I couldn't even see her with my third eye.

"Are you going to tell anyone about us?" he asked warily.

"No, I won't tell anyone who will hurt you. I will probably tell my family about you, but they are good people and won't hurt you," I told him.

Teluke obviously wasn't inclined to give me the benefit of the doubt and was adamant that I not tell anyone at all! However, I knew my husband's family and felt I could trust them.

"You can't stay here," he told me firmly. I politely told him that I came here for healing and that I would stay for a bit.

I sat there soaking in the beauty of the woods when Teluke, apparently wanting to hurry things along, sent into me a surge of energy that enveloped me in love and a sense of fullness and well being, which brought me to tears. Again, he told me to leave.

On the conscious level, all I could figure him to be was something like the tree spirits that used to haunt my windows at dust, looking for me when I was a child. (Before judging my sanity, realize the cultural difference of perception of Native Americans and that of the dominant culture.)

I refused to leave and told him once again to just ignore me, because I couldn't see them anyway, and would mind my own business.

In a pleading voice he explained, "You don't understand! We can't stay this way (meaning invisible) too long! We just had a baby. My mate isn't well and I am trying to heal her."

My instincts took over.

"Is there anything I can do to help you?" I asked.

Abruptly, he said, "Yes! Leave!"

I was real annoyed at this point. My offerings of help and goodwill were denied, and this invisible being wanted me out of the woods when I badly needed the repose. I had intended to stay for a good half-hour or so, and had only been there maybe five minutes, tops. I wasn't bothering anyone, but every time I would get busy day dreaming and minding my own business, something in their direction would catch my peripheral vision. I would turn to look at them, only to startle them and have them blink out of visible sight again. This annoyed him as well as me. He told me I was NOT minding my own business, and I insisted I was.

I told him that observing them was no different than watching the trees and squirrels. He didn't agree with me at all and again he ordered me to leave.

When I refused, he said, "Then I will make you leave!"

Immediately, I felt like my head imploded and I grabbed it with my hands. I then felt as though someone other than me was operating my legs, independent of me from inside! My legs lifted me to my feet and I yelled, "What are you doing?" to which he replied very simply, "Making you leave."

I was physically pulled a few yards in the direction from which I had entered the woods and said, "OK! But I'm going out the other side!"

The force let go momentarily and he said, "If you do, then don't come back through here!"

I told him I intended to do so, and that I would have to. He retorted, "Then you are going out the same way you came in!"

Who did he think he was, anyway? It wasn't his woods. I had as much right to use the woods as anyone!

The result was a tug-of-war on my "ignorant vessel", as we took turns asserting our will upon it. I would lose ground when he had the upper hand and gain ground when I caught his will off guard. At one point I found myself tromping through what obviously was their toilet area at the foot of the stream. I was totally frustrated by trying to hold my concentration to enable me to cross the woods. Occasionally he would say, "You are wasting my time!" (my translation).

To which I would reply, "Then, leave me alone! I'm not hurting anything!"

The disorientation was so great, and trying to hold my concentration was so difficult, my head felt like it was splitting open and I became nauseous. At some point my confusion was so great, that I totally forgot what I was attempting to do. I realized I had been walking for a long time, seemingly in circles, and never seemed to find the edge of the woods. My objective then changed to just finding my way out! I came out exactly where I had entered the woods. I turned around to face the woods, totally confused on the conscious level, and my Second Attention heard, "And don't come back!"

It took me fifteen years to realize why I had gotten lost in that stinking little woodlot, when I can walk for hours in large unfamiliar forests and never get lost!

# ❧ CHAPTER TWO ❧

## The Gravity of it All

*"…Abandoned thought in full array*

*escapes a child in light of day*

*from truth that one would rarely want*

*that nay returns the innocent"*

TOTALLY DISGUSTED FROM HAVING BEEN ushered out of the woods by something invisible, I wiped the dung off my boots and went inside the house. My Mother-in-law asked how my walk was. I told her that the strangest thing had happened. That I had walked up on what looked like a bear, asleep beside a log. I told her that it jumped up and totally disappeared! I also said that someone was living in the woods. She asked me who and I told her I didn't know for sure. I explained that the woods definitely looked lived in, and that I saw where they go to the bathroom all the time.

This concerned her, thinking it may be a tramp, and she said she had better tell Pop about it when he came home. Instantly the Sasquatch astral projected himself into the room. He had been listening and he was furious with me!

"I told you not to tell ANYONE! Now I have to take care of it! You'll pay for this! I am going to destroy you!" he leered at me.

Part of me was terrified at who this being was that could enter the house at will, to get at me. My Christian thoughts, at that time, would only entertain it to be some kind of demon. I begged Mom not to tell Pop. Trying to soften things, I told her that it was a man and his wife and that she had just had a baby. I told her I had found the placenta and that they just wanted to be left alone!

Mom was shocked about them having had a baby out in the woods and she asked if she needed a doctor. I told her that he was a doctor and Mom wanted to know why they were living in the woods. Were they criminals or something?

I explained then that they just didn't like the way society lived and they wanted to be left alone. Mom certainly agreed with them on this and asked what they were eating. I told her the man knew plants real well. She wondered if there was enough out there for them to eat and offered me some canned food to take out to them.

I said that they probably could use food, but that I didn't believe they would eat from cans. Besides not having a can opener, they would then have garbage lying around in the woods, which was precisely what they didn't want. I suggested that they might however, appreciate some fresh produce from the garden.

Later in the afternoon I began feeling quite ill. When Pop came home from work, I was well on the way to the first and only migraine headache I've ever had. Mom told Pop about the incident and wanted him to go check out the woods.

I was keenly aware that the Sasquatch was at the woods edge all day watching for Pop to come home. The Sasquatch had acknowledged his presence to me there as well as his vengeful intentions whenever I had checked to see.

So it was with consternation that I saw Teluke, with my Second Attention, telescope his astral body into the kitchen between Mom and Pop! They both took a step backwards. Pop was just about to reply to Mom, when they both turned to look at Teluke. Apparently, Teluke realized he was being pretty obvious, because he blinked back out of visible sight. Pop was caught off guard and laughed, "Ha! For a second, I thought there was a man standing there." Mom agreed that she too had seen him and they tried to remember what they were talking about before the incident.

Pop gave the response I had pretty much expected from him, which was to live and let live, let them be, but I have no way of knowing for sure whether the Sasquatch man induced this reply or not.

Shortly thereafter, my migraine was so unbearable that I had tunnel vision amd even darkness was horribly painful to me. I was told that going for a walk and inducing oneself to vomit would relieve it. I went outside to the pasture fence and vomited. My ignorant physical body glanced up to the woods, disbelieving that anyone could wish this unbelievable pain on someone. I also began to realize the full weight of the situation and just how easily things could snowball out of hand.

I went into the house to go to my bedroom and lie on the bed. Zanna inspired me with a dream in which I could see one person telling another, until some gang of well-meaning folks were tromping through the woods with guns. And, if Sasquatch truly cannot stay invisible for very long, they could somehow get cornered in that tiny woods and be harmed.

I knew I could not live with that on my conscience and I became protective of them, deciding to keep my mouth shut from now on. My husband was a consideration to tell only for a moment. Although he was outwardly fascinated with the "Bigfoot" phenomenon, previous experience proved, (and also when I introduced him to the Star People) that he was much too frightened at a deep level, to be able to deal with something this physical on any conscious level. In fact, what he carried unconsciously about it all eventually began to weaken the foundation of our marriage and set in motion a psychological rejection and distrust of me.

I also discovered there was more to it than just keeping my mouth shut. It was much too easy to speak in reference to the

Sasquatch, explaining away all the little mysteries that began cropping up. Several times I slipped up and had to dig my way out fast. For instance, yelling at the Collie to leave "him" alone, and having to explain exactly who I was talking about, when others were around to hear me. Eventually, I put my foot in it royally, and had to lie (which I'm not good at) in such an obvious way that it was apparent to everyone I was keeping a secret. A big one. An important one.

My girlfriend Nan, asked me point blank what I was up to. She was concerned and knew I was keeping something to myself. She mentioned I had been acting pretty weird lately and that she had even spoken to Mom about me, who was also concerned. Later Mom cornered me as well, wanting to know if everything was all right.

No! Everything was not all right! I had a great responsibility, which if not handled discreetly and carefully, could end in tragedy. I was making too many careless mistakes. I knew something had to be done fast. I searched inside myself until I drew upon old knowledge that I hadn't used for many lifetimes.

I split my consciousness into a working order that allowed me full awareness of the facts involved, then forced myself to store the reality up so far into an attic corner of my waking consciousness that I would only allow my conscious thoughts to turn towards the Sasquatch when I was totally alone. The power to do this was located at my center, my solar plexus.

It was a deliberate and handy trick, and it felt good to exercise it again. Therefore, I could remain just as perplexed, surprised and ignorant on the conscious level as everyone else when strange things happened, such as a bucket being knocked over, or the swing being bumped, or the dogs going nuts. Only when I was completely alone, would I then allow the true acknowledgment to drip down into my consciousness like a leaky faucet. The key to my conscious mind was the constant hunger pangs to be alone, just as a good book nags at you to get back to it.

Soon after the baby was born, I telepathed up to the woods to the Sasquatch family, that we had bought a cake and celebrated the birth of their baby (explaining to them that no one was aware of it). They were surprised and thanked me for it.

I would constantly find myself outside gazing up the field to the woods. The horses had stopped grazing the last half of the pasture up near the woods also. I walked out there to the force field which Teluke had set up, several time a day to wish them well, tell them I loved them, and to see if there was anything I could get for them or help them in any way.

After a number of trips out there, due to Zanna's prompting, Teluke got tired of me.

"Are you back again? My people told me you people are trouble. Now I see what they mean! Please, just leave us alone. We don't want any trouble. I am just a man who wants to take care of his family. We haven't been here long and you already want to start trouble!" he said.

I was hurt and shocked by his words. I didn't mean any harm, only support! I had no intention of making trouble! But I realized it sounded like he was inexperienced with our people and knew only what he had heard about us.

"Haven't you ever seen our people before?" I asked him.

"No!" he said.

I couldn't imagine anyone having lived in the United States and being able to stay isolated that much! I told him that he had as much to learn about us as I hoped to learn about them.

My heart was anguished. What a wonderful opportunity I had here and was being denied access to. I told him that my husband and I had always been fascinated about them and that it was important that we establish a workable system of communication between us so we could all benefit.

Teluke shot out, "What did you just say?"

I repeated it.

"You aren't even talking! You're not saying anything at all!" he said. "You people are so stupid! You are not using words at all!" he continued. He was quite insulting about it.

I tried to explain that there are many ways of speaking on earth, but he seemed quite self-righteous about my having a bigger vocabulary, most of which he had never heard before.

This caused me to reassess our differences in language, and because his communications were so extremely basic, I made the mistake of reevaluating his intelligence, likening him to the mildly retarded, or possibly a five year old child with limited understanding. With this came a feeling of graciousness on my part, coming "down" to his level to facilitate his deficiency, and I began speaking a sort of pigeon-English.

To him, my people and I were the ignorant ones, and I was just making up words. He immediately sensed my arrogant feelings of superiority, even though well intended, and shot back accusingly, "You think we're stupid!"

I assured him I did not, but that I was merely trying to facilitate our communications, then realizing my choice of words, restated that I wanted us to better understand each other.

He assured me he was capable of understanding, but that we were stupid for making up words. Yet, when I used pigeon-English, he felt insulted as well. We agreed that I would speak in my own words and he would ask what certain words meant, providing I would not think less of him for asking. I assured him that asking questions was a sure sign of "being smart". So with his keen memory, recalling where this all started, he asked me what "husband" was.

I told him it was the man I live with. He asked if it was my mate and I acknowledged that it was.

"Well, why don't you just say mate, then?" he asked. "Husband is a stupid word" and then he wanted to know what Byron's word for me was. I told him I am his wife and he liked that word. He tried it out a few times and said that some of our words were good and he would use that one. But in all, he remained indignant and made it clear that he had had enough of me for one day. So, I apologized and left.

That night before bed, as I tucked myself under the covers, I telepathed to them "goodnight" and they said "goodnight" to me as well. It was good to know I could reach them, even from my house, day or night.

# CHAPTER THREE

*Awkward Availabilities*

"...new garments adorn the body

invisible to all of life as they know it.

Reality reverses poles

and the world blinks off..."

THE FOLLOWING MORNING I HUNG around the pasture gate like a dieter around a refrigerator, desperately wanting my freedom to visit, but knowing better. I didn't want to bother them, which obviously my good intentions were doing.

I brushed out the Collie and began to play with him. The dog was mouthing my arm when suddenly my head felt like it was going to explode from an incredible force within!

It was Teluke. My immediate thoughts were, "My God! What is this?" I didn't really expect an answer, since I didn't know what it was to begin with. But, just as painfully, the answer came as Teluke identified himself. I yelled at him in my thoughts, to not speak so loudly, as it was causing me unbearable pain!

He came back softer with, "How is this?" But it was still much too loud. Four times I had him lower his volume until it was comfortable for me. I told him he just didn't need to apply any extra effort to speak to me, because I was 'right here', meaning just as telepathically close to them as they were to me.

I asked him where he was, and he said he was up in the woods. He wanted to know if that dog was biting me. I told him that we were playing.

"But he had his mouth on your arm!" he exclaimed. Again, it was apparent that his contact with the outside world was minimal. I explained that since dogs don't have hands like we do, they use their mouths to hold things instead.

"Doesn't it hurt you?" Teluke asked.

I told him that it wasn't really comfortable (then re-explaining in simpler words that it didn't feel real good), but the dog was being as gentle and as soft as he could be. I told him the teeth leave bruises and then had to explain what bruises were.

He then wanted to know what I was doing with him earlier over there on the ground. I explained I was brushing him out. He wanted to know why, and I told him it was because I loved the dog and brushing keeps his skin healthy. Teluke said, "That is good to take care of those you love."

Seeing this as an opportunity to interact, I offered to brush him out as well, which he resentfully declined. After a moment's pause, in which he collected himself, he continued the conversation.

"Dogs give my people a lot of trouble," he said. (I realize most reports state that dogs refuse to enter the woods of a Sasquatch or trail them, but this is what he said to me. Our own dogs barked but were not always terrified, possibly due to their being in the other dimension.)

I offered to teach him about dogs. We exchanged telepathic pictures of dogs and he showed me a coon dog. I told him they were a breed I had not had first-hand experience with, but had seen in action on TV.

He wanted to know what TV was, so I explained that a main station somewhere sends out energy, and in our homes we have boxes that receive pictures and sound. This box talks so we can see and hear things that happen far away. He didn't believe me, so I told him he could come up to the house at night and look in our windows to see it for himself.

"My people told me you have a lot of magic!" he said in awe.

I told him we call it an "idiot box". I said that on Friday nights the family goes to the store and I usually go with them. I suggested that I could stay home and he could come up for a visit and I would show him our house.

He didn't know what "Friday" was and said that we use strange words. So, I patiently explained how we have the year broken down into months, weeks, days. I told him that today was Wednesday and tomorrow, when the sun comes up again, it would be Thursday. I then said that the next sun-up would be Friday and when it gets dark on that day, to come up to the house after he sees the car leave. I asked if he understood and would he remember. He became indignant again, and said we think his people are stupid. He stated emphatically that he remembers everything I tell him!

I was ashamed, but I had to admit to myself that I had indeed thought of him in lower terms, as if he were simply a smart ape. I explained that I simply did not know anything about his people. I said that it would be just as rude for me to assume that he understood everything I talked about. I told him that I wished to learn about his people and that he could learn from me as well.

He asked why we use so many words and I told him that my people seem to feel that the more words you use, the smarter you must be. And, they do it not only to clarify their thoughts, but often to impress other people as well.

He said to me that words don't make you smarter. I agreed with him and said that it was a stupid thing we people do to gain acceptance and feel important. I further explained that just because I know some words that he doesn't know, it doesn't make me better or smarter than he is. I told him that his people are better at some things than we are, just as my people may be better at some things than they.

I looked around in the sky. "See that bird up there flying around?" I asked.

"Well, he can fly, but I can't. That doesn't make him better than me. It only makes him different than me. I can run across the ground and ride a horse, but the bird can't. He is better at flying. I am better at riding a horse. Neither is greater, both are good," I said.

He liked that. "You said that good. I like birds," he said.

His very simple purity was always touching me. Such child-like perception is refreshing to come across in our very complicated world. I wished that it would rub off on to me before our time together was at an end. But, as with all things, there is a positive and a negative side, and his distaste for my people continued to surface. He seemed to like pointing out our differences in a very judgmental way.

"My people have good bodies!" he said. 'You people lie!', 'You people take everything and leave us nothing!'; 'You people can't run!', ' We are stronger!' etc. Though most of it was true, it was irritating to constantly be reminded of one's shortcomings. I often tried to get him to lower his shield by explaining that, " I have more respect for others and to give me a chance." Where I was watching for our sameness, he looked for differences and I pointed out his bigotry.

"Bigotry," I explained, "is when one kind of people think they are better than another and disapprove of their differences. For instance, one color of people hates another color, then it builds into hating each other because someone doesn't believe the same way you do, and it just goes on and on until the whole world hates itself. You don't like me because I have a weaker body and you can do so much more with yours. My Mother used to tell me that God gave everything He created, a way to protect itself. Some of us He gave antlers or horns; some of us have fast feet, some of us have big teeth or sharp claws to protect ourselves. He gave you strength and nice fur, but he didn't give my people any of those things! What He gave us was a brain to think ourselves out of trouble. We make our own protection with intelligence," I told him.

"Your Mother is a smart female," he said. "Not like you! I would like to meet your Mother. I bet she is sad she had you!" he said, pointedly.

How many times I had felt this myself. I couldn't argue with him. His words struck deeply and I broke down and wept, silently.

"What are you doing?" he questioned.

"I am crying," I told him.

"Why?" he mused.

"Because you hurt me," I answered him.

"I never touched you!" he bellowed.

"Yes, you did. Your words touched me and they hurt," I answered.

"Oh, how can words touch you?" he queried.

I started to explain, but decided just to call it quits for now and go inside.

Later, when I went out to feed the animals, he asked me if I would come up closer to the woods so he could look at me. I was delighted to get the chance to get closer to him. He stopped me about 20 feet from the fence.

"What do you have on your body, and what do you have on your head?" he asked. "It looks stupid! You people look stupid!" he continued.

Embarrassed, I looked around to see what I had on that looked stupid. Generally, that would mean I had a three foot string of toilet paper stuck to my boot, but I quickly realized he was speaking of my clothes and cowboy hat.

Feeling self-conscious, I removed my "stupid looking" hat and explained they were clothing.

"Why do you have them on?" he asked.

"Because we don't have beautiful hair on our bodies like you do and we need to protect ourselves so we don't get sunburned," I told him.

"What is 'sunburned'?" he inquired.

"That is when the sun makes our skin hot and red and hurt," I explained. "The sun makes our skin blister and come off if we don't protect it. Our clothes also keep us warm in cold weather since we do not have a natural coat like you. If we did not wear clothes we would die of exposure," I told him.

"What is exposure?" Teluke asked warily. He seemed unsure if I wasn't just making all this up.

"We would die from being naked, from not having protection," I said. "We also wear clothes because we have rules that say we must. People, men mostly, won't leave other peoples' bodies alone sexually, if we are naked," I continued.

Teluke was disgusted at this and had heard of this before. He commented on our crude sexuality, and then asked me to turn around, which I did freely.

"You people look stupid!" he reaffirmed. It was obvious that whoever had told him about our people didn't care too much for us and had probably been harassed. I did not feel his opinion was at all based on his personal experience, but was a perception probably borrowed from someone who had been given a pretty hard time by us. It was totally based on the apprehension of a people he did not know personally, and about whom he had only heard bad things said. It was based on fear.

Feeling rather at loose ends, having been verbally abused, I asked him if he would let me see him. He stepped out into the clearing a bit, but remained well back from the fence. He was invisible to the eye, but I didn't notice this since I picked him up with my Second Attention.

With all of his distaste of me, I felt obligated to be just as honest with my opinions of his appearance. "Well, you don't look so great yourself!" I chided. "Your head is pointed, you don't even have a neck! You look top-heavy and you're built like a gorilla!" I had to laugh at who was calling 'the kettle black'. He had every right to feel just as awkward about his appearance as he had made me feel. He was just as different from me as I was from him.

He was appalled that a female would dare talk to him that way. I felt Teleel, his mate, gasp and hold her breath in suspense. I could telepathically see him internally visualizing his appearance.

"We have good bodies! What is gorilla?" he asked me.

"Gorilla is a big monkey," I explained. "Do you know what a monkey is?" I wasn't trying to be insulting as much as I was just being honest.

"Yes, we know of such things. I am **not** a monkey! I am a **human being** just like **you**!" he said loudly. He was truly offended by this, but no more so than I was at his remarks.

He was such a splendid mixture of man and ape, it occurred to me that they might inter-breed. I asked him if this were so.

"No! We do not mate with animals!" he said. "That is wrong. Do you people?" he countered.

"No, we don't," I replied. Then, as an after thought I added, "Well, most of us don't, but there are a few 'sick-os' out there that will do anything!" I said with disgust.

Teluk's eyes got wide in contempt and he turned his head to the side to include Teleel. "Did you hear that? They mate with animals!" he said with disgust.

"Yes, I heard!" she said incredulously.

How cleverly and quickly he had turned the tables. Now I had to talk fast.

"I told you no!" I said in defense. "We know it is wrong too, and so we don't. It's just sometimes people get sick in their heads and if they do this we do not approve or accept this action," I said.

His only response was to tell me to go away now, which I was glad to do.

For the next couple of nights, I felt his presence outside the house. The house was in the country and the back of the house was private so we didn't worry too much about prowlers. One night while I was getting undressed in the bathroom, I noticed Teluke peering in the window at me. It made me angry and I pulled the curtain closed.

Telepathically, he asked me what we do in 'there'. I explained that we clean our bodies and relieve ourselves in here, and we consider it a private thing. I told him not to peek in this window, but he could look in the other windows. He said that there was something in the way in the other rooms and couldn't see very well. I realized that Mom, who changed the furniture around every week, had placed a chair and sofa in front of the windows, blocking his view. I explained this to him and said to be patient, she would change it again very soon and then he would be able to see in.

Meanwhile, he frightened my sister-in-law when she caught him peeking in at her. She screamed for Pop. Pop charged outside and around the house. When he came in, he had mixed feelings. He sort of laughed beneath his anger and said he had scared him off down the lane, "but not before a skunk got to him."

I began to feel uncomfortable with Teluke's pompous attitude, so one day I sneaked out into the pasture, keeping my thoughts to myself so I would not be detected by him. I wanted to have a pleasant girl chat with his mate, my old acquaintance, Teleel.

"Sweetie, are you there?" I asked quietly.

"Yes, I am here," came her soft feminine voice telepathically.

"Would you like to 'girl talk' a little while?" I felt her anticipation to my questions.

"Yes! I miss having a female to talk to," she answered.

I was glad she was anxious to share. "How are you feeling? And, how is the baby?" I asked her.

"Are you still bleeding badly or hurting?" I asked, concerned because it had only been a couple of weeks since she gave birth.

"No, I am feeling good," she said. " My mate takes good care of me. I am almost back to.... how I was before," she replied softly.

I was surprised to hear this. "Really? Golly, my people hurt for a long time after a baby is born. You <u>must</u> have better bodies than we do!" I told her.

"Yes," she said, "we have good bodies!"

I continued, feeling like an old nurse-maid. "How is your milk, honey? Do you have plenty for the baby?"

"Yes. My milk is good. The baby is growing fast," she answered enthusiastically. The sound of her voice had such pleasure to it. I could sense her pride. I felt like an old woman sitting there in the alfalfa field.

"I wish I knew my plants. I used to know all of the plants! But, this body has never learned them. I would like to take care of you," I told her.

"Thank you. But my mate takes good care of me," she answered.

"Have you been married long?" I asked her, forgetting we had a vocabulary gap since she was so easy to talk to.

"What is 'married'?" she asked. I explained this to her.

"No, not too long," she answered.

"Do you like being mated?" I felt the need to know if she was happy.

"Yes, he is good to me most of the time," she said.

Still feeling like the 'old matriarch', I inquired further. "Does Teluke make love to you often?" Telepathically, I felt her blush and saw her hide her face in her hands at my being so personal.

She giggled. "Well, not too often. Our men are not like your men, who hurt their women that way," There was no racial prejudice in her tone as there generally was with Teluke. I felt so happy for her.

"Oh, that is good," I said. "I am so glad to hear that! So you enjoy him this way, then?" I asked.

She giggled again, "Yes,"

I thoroughly enjoyed the private girl talk as I knew she did too, since she had no one but Teluke to talk to now.

# CHAPTER FOUR

## Deficient Contacts

*"…even as I drew each  breath the creative*

*forces within the atmosphere paid homage*

*to the Deity by reinforcing within me*

*The New Creation…"*

W HEN FRIDAY CAME, I WONDERED all day if Teluke would show up. When evening finally arrived I felt him prowling around outside the living room windows. The scrappy little housedog attacked the curtains furiously, so I quickly called him out into the kitchen for a "goodie" to distract the family from Teluke. But, the dog wolfed down the goodie and ran back to the windows, barking wildly. All I could do was make merriment of it and exclaim that he "sure doesn't want the family to leave tonight! See what a good dog he is? Can I go? Can I go?" I mimicked in a teeny chicken sort of voice.

Shortly afterward, the family left for the store and I paced the floor nervously, like an anxious teenager waiting for her first date. No sooner had the car pulled out of the driveway, when two loud bangs on the back door broke the silence of the vacuum my racing heart had created. I ran to the back door and opened it, thoroughly delighted.

With my third eye, I saw a hairy, boyish creature with an impish grin, standing down the steps. He stepped backwards, creating a half bent stance as he swung his right leg behind him. He appeared quite the sport!

Again, I felt like an old matriarch. "Well, good evening!" I said. "Don't you look sporty tonight! I am so honored that you came to visit me. Won't you please come in?" I asked him.

Teluke jumped backwards in surprise. "No," he responded.

Feeling very obliging, I stepped outside. "Well, that is quite all right. I will come out and sit on the step to visit with you!" I said. I could see he was still quite taken back by me for some reason.

"Can you see me? Why aren't you afraid of me?" he asked wide-eyed. All of this was new to him, and he wasn't used to being so obviously detected and confronted this way.

"I can't see you with my eyes, but I can see you quite well another way," I told him. "I have never seen a more pure being!" I continued, "Your people are so easy to read, you are so pure. There is nothing in you to be afraid of!" I assured him. "I can see your heart and there is no evil in it. I see a great deal of fear though, and I wish to help you eliminate that."

He stood there listening, enthralled. "You people can see into our bodies? You can see my heart?" he asked.

I laughed delightedly. "No, sweetie, I can't see into your body," I explained. "I see your spirit, the real you inside your body and it is pure light."

I could see he was relaxing a bit as he looked around and asked, "Aren't you afraid someone will see you sitting out here?"

I assured him that people often sit on the steps at night to enjoy a pleasant evening and watch the stars. "Would you like to come into the house and look around?" I asked. "There is no one home now. I will leave the door open for you," I reassured. I did so want him to come within my walls.

"Don't you have a dog in there?" he asked me.

"Oh, that's right! Just a minute and I will lock him in the bathroom so he can't get at you," I said, and excused myself.

On returning, I was disgusted at my attire for such a special event. I needed my regalia and jewelry of long ago. I was so honored. I touched my hair up with my hand as I opened the door for Teluke to enter my home. Teluke darted past me and on into the kitchen. The floor creaked under his weight as he entered the room. I left the inside door open, but the storm door automatically shut itself, and I didn't know what else to do but let it and go on in with my guest.

He asked me what the table and chairs were. I could see he was extremely nervous and I wondered if the old floor would hold him. Assessing the situation, I understood that if I sat down, it would possibly calm him down some, so I sat down and explained the furniture to him.

He asked why we use it and I said that it is hard for our old people to get all the way down to the ground and get back up, so they use chairs. And since children are around them, they also use them and soon we are being raised to use furniture.

Just then the television blurted out and startled Teluke. "I thought you said we were alone!" he accused me wide-eyed.

I smiled and told him that we are alone and that was the television of which I had told him about. I coaxed him into the living room to see it for his self. What a different side of him I was seeing in this frightened boy from the confident strong man I visited in the woods. He was totally out of his element.

He stepped into the living room and glanced around quickly, then stared at the TV. "It really is magic! It talks!" he said totally fascinated.

Just then a car went by the picture window and blew its horn, sending Teluke into a panic. He was at the back door in a blur. He smashed into the storm door and was about to beat it down. He looked at me, wild-eyed in disbelief at finding himself trapped and betrayed. "You said it would be open!" he demanded.

I ran yelling after him, "It's okay! Don't break it! Don't break it! I'll let you out!"

"You said it would be open!" he accused me again as I opened it.

As he flew out the door, I begged him to let me explain that the door shuts by itself, and I demonstrated it for him. I told him that I left the inside door open for him!

He said he would never trust me again. I tried to explain that I meant he would be free to leave, that I would not hold him there.

"Then why didn't you say that? he asked. "You people twist your words around, how do you understand each other? I was told you people lie, but I trusted you!"

I told him that we look at the situation. I said that if I told him that my door was always open to them, they might come to my house and find the door shut, but they should know that I meant that if they ever needed food or shelter, they could use my house as their own. I explained that I had spoken to him in a way that my own people would have understood.

He asked me then, "You would let me and my family use your place?"

I assured him that I would, if this were my own home. But since it belonged to my mate's family and was not mine, I was not free to do that. However, I would help them as much as possible.

I could see that it was too late for apologies. I had damaged his faith in me. He turned away and said, "I will never trust you again! My people told me you people lie!"

I worried all night and through the next day about regaining his trust. I spoke to Zanna who was always available to me, and she said she would try to help me.

Mom was cleaning fresh vegetables in the double sink at our country home, when the phone rang. Mom talked for a while and then returned to her work. She said that the neighbor reported having seen a man standing in the living room while they were away shopping. I could feel her questions surfacing about my loyalty to her son. I assured her it could only have been me they had seen. She accepted my honesty and pleasantly resumed cleaning the vegetables, when out of the blue she was inspired to offer me some leftover scraps for the people living in the woods, if I thought they might like them. I could see she hadn't connected the two subjects.

It was just what I needed. I was grateful and thanked her as I scooped up the scraps and carried them out through the pasture. I asked Zanna if this was her idea and she confirmed it. She had planted the idea in Mom's mind.

"I have brought you some food," I telepathed to the woods. I felt their hearts rise. "Thank you. Lay it down and go away. I will come and get it. Did you poison it?" asked Teluke.

"Poison? Why would I ever do anything like that?" I asked, totally dumb-founded. "Of course not. I wouldn't do that!" I said.

"Why are you being so nice?" he asked suspiciously.

"Because I love you," I replied

"Well, you people poison food and make us sick all the time," he responded. "Lay it down and go!"

I was disheartened that he stopped me at the force field, but not surprised.

"I can bring it up to the fence so no one will see you come out to get it," I said.

It still wasn't established consciously that I did not see them with my eyes. The conversations and the whole interaction was so tucked away on my Second Attention, that I didn't allow myself to draw on its reference. If someone had come up to me right then and asked me what I was doing, I would not have had an answer for them. On the conscious level, I would have felt anxiety, mixed with fear and been utterly confused to find myself out in the pasture with food, and I would have rationalized some answer that I could half-way believe myself. The fear factor did eventually readjust itself more comfortably with my conscious mind later on.

Teluke assured me that no one would see him come get the food, so I reluctantly laid down my arm load of cabbage leaves and carrot tops and asked if they needed anything else.

"Do you have salt?" he asked in a tone as if he deserved it for my having lied to him.

Good! This was something else I could do. "Sure!" I said. "There are salt blocks up in the paddock," I pointed. "You can sneak up there at night, so no one will see you, and take some, but don't take all of it because the horses need some also."

"Aren't there dogs up there, too?" he asked suspiciously.

"Yes, but he is always on the chain," I answered. "There is also some food in the garden," again pointing. "If you don't take too much from one place, or too much at one time, I am sure no one will miss it. Just spread it around some," I said. I was glad to be able to help them.

"Thank you. Now go," Teluke said.

I turned and walked away a few steps and glanced back to see the fence bow over as he stepped over it. It annoyed him and I giggled.

I left them alone for a few days. When I went back out to check on them, he didn't answer me right away. Suddenly he yelled, "I thought you said those dogs were tied up!" His voice boomed with strength.

Panic stricken, I answered, "They are!" I was frantic at this accusation. I could feel something was really wrong.

"That one over there is not!" he directed. "He chased me all the way to the fence and you watched and laughed!"

Oh, my dear Lord! He was right! I had been in the yard with other people and didn't fully allow myself to realize what was going on. I had thought it was humorous because that particular dog was harmless. He was running just for the sport of having something run from him. Now I was really in a tough spot! Two grave mistakes. I couldn't imagine ever overcoming these odds with him being so distrustful to begin with.

He had told me that I was the first of my people he had dealt with. We both had so much to learn about each other and I was losing ground I couldn't afford.

"Oh, dear Lord!" I cried out. "I am so sorry! I forgot about the Collie! I was talking about the dog at the barn. He is the one that will bite! The other one is only tied up at night," I said.

"Why do you keep it if it bites?" he asked, though it was more of a statement than a question.

"We keep him to keep people from stealing the horses," I explained. "I am so sorry! I totally forgot about the other dog because he is so friendly. He wasn't even a consideration. I would tie him up if he was my dog, but he is not."

An idea came to me. "Maybe when you see me out in the yard, you could let me know you wish to come up for food and I could put him up for a few minutes, or hold him while you use the garden. He really is friendly! I could teach you about dogs," I said.

"Yes!" Teluke made the words sound like an order. "I will let you teach me about dogs and everything about your people. There will be a great war! My people will come and kill your people! We have talked of this before!"

My heart saddened at this idea. These beautiful beings were not turning out to be what I had always known in my heart that they were.

You may come to kill us, but I will not war with you or join my people against you," I answered. "I do not believe in war and hate. I will teach you how you may protect yourselves from dogs though. We can start now, if you would like."

Teluke said it was okay with him, so I stretched out in the tall hay and began.

"When you run, you give the dog something fun to chase. You can't outrun a dog," I began.

Teluke broke in caustically, "I can outrun any dog!"

"I'm sure you can," I said quickly. "I am telling you the rules my people follow."

I explained that the Collie was thinking in terms of, "Oh, Boy! Oh, Boy! Me too!" and that the dog was wanting to play and have fun. I told him that rarely will a dog actually bite if you stand your ground and face the dog. Never turn your back to him. I said that some dogs know certain words like no; stay; down; bad dog; good boy, etc. I told him that they do understand some words and to try to talk to the Collie.

I went on to say that they reflect what you expect from them because they read your mind more than most people realize. "So, if you expect a dog to be mean, he will most likely think he is supposed to be mean," I said. I told him if he would try this, the Collie would likely come right up to him, barking, but I could almost promise that the dog would not bite him.

I made a point to explain that I could not fully promise the actions of any other being, but I know this dog to be a sweet personality. Then I went on to explain the body language of dogs and the different breed personalities. After about an hour, Teluke said that was enough for one time and for me to go now.

"I really am terribly sorry about this. It was an honest mistake. I really do love you so," I emphasized, then turned and walked away.

I was pleased with the session and hoped I had regained at least some ground, somewhere. At least I was still interacting with him. I had put out a lot of good information in a nice amount of time. I was sure it would be very useful to him at some point in his life.

Zanna felt bad for me, but warned me not to let anything else happen! She said she would try to help me get his interest back.

Note:I will not apologize for the seeming discrepancy of how our dogs reacted to these Sasquatch from the majority of Bigfoot reports with dogs being terrified. It could very possibly be that they were not as terrified as most hunting dogs are reported to be when encountering B.F., because of the interdimensionality in progress. I can't explain it. I can only report it. If I was making this up I would conform to these reports.

# ᴄ Chapter Five ᴄ

## Caustic Impacts

*"…Moreover the soul shall comprehend*

*that things of earth do not depend*

*upon the force of mans invent*

*but on the love of hearts content."*

A DAY OR SO LATER I heard him telepath for me to get the dog because he was coming up for food. Mom was out in the yard hanging up clothes. I put old "Charlie-Bill" on his chain and opened the pasture gate by the garden. What happened next was so unbelievable to me that I was appalled at the position I was being put in! Mom started hollering, "Look at the garden!"

Dirt was flying everywhere! Vegetables were plucking themselves out of the ground and throwing themselves into a pile! It looked like a Bugs Bunny cartoon!

I thought, "Oh, shit! What the hell is he doing? How am I going to explain this?" Teluke was in his transparent form so all one could see was the result of his movements. It was such an absurd scene I couldn't help but fold over with laughter. But, at the same time I had to convince Mom that I didn't see anything and that what she was seeing wasn't real!

Mom was just a hollering and holding her heart. "Well, would you look at that! Now it's over there in the cabbages! This can't be happening, but there it is! You see that don't you?" she cried out. "Oh, my heart. It's just a beatin'. I think I'm having a heart attack! I really do, now! This can't be happening. Those vegetables are just a pluckin' themselves right up out of the ground and throwing themselves into a pile! Don't be tellin' me you don't see that! Look at that! Dirt's a flyin' everywhere. Oh, my heart!"

I was beside myself laughing at this ridiculous sight and trying to convince Mom that of course it is impossible, therefore she wasn't seeing anything. I kept repeating, when I could speak at all, "No, I don't see anything, Mom. See what? What are you talking about?"

I could hear the Sasquatch's thoughts: "I hope she does die! I'll take as much of their food as I want!"

And, if that wasn't enough, the whole pile of food then picked itself up and floated in saucy bounces out into the pasture! I sent Teluke my thoughts, "You don't have to be so damn saucy, or I'll kick your ass from here!" I felt him glare at me, but he didn't respond.

That was just about all poor Mom's heart could stand as her voice raised to a crescendo. "Oh, my God! And lookie there, would you! I don't cuss like this, but, I believe I have to for this! Lookie! Them vegetables are just a floatin' themselves right out to the pasture. Now you see that? Don't tell me you don't. That can't happen! But, right there it is! Oh, my heart! I think I'm through for the day. I'm gonna have to go in and lie down!"

"Of course it can't happen, Mom. Are you gonna be alright?" I asked, trying to soothe her as I ushered her into the house. I was totally amused, but frustrated.

I knew Teluke was feeling self-righteous, so I waited a day or so before I paid him a visit concerning the whole affair. I wanted it clear that I meant business.

"Hey, you! I want to talk to you!" I telepathed.

"Go away! I don't want to talk to you!" he retorted.

"No, you are going to hear me out! You knew Mom was out there in the yard, but you waltzed right in and made a perfect spectacle of yourself and left me holding the bag!"

"What bag?" he asked.

"You put me in the awkward position of having to explain everything that she saw," I explained. "It was so ridiculous to see

52

dirt flying everywhere, and vegetables flying through the air to land in a pile, that I couldn't keep from laughing! But at the same time, I had to convince Mom that it wasn't real and that she wasn't actually seeing it happen! You have to understand that my people, as a general rule, think that if you can't see it, it isn't real!"

"Go away! We aren't real," Teluke broke in. I heard them both giggle.

"Give me a break will you?" I was exasperated.

"Go away! We aren't real!" Again they both giggled. I had to join them with a chuckle, but went on with my dissertation. "And, if going through that once wasn't enough, I had to go through it again at supper time when she told the family and she asked me to back her up. Just the thought of what I saw kept a stupid grin on my face, and I had to lie again, and say that I didn't see anything! I'm not a liar! I'm not good at it, and I don't approve of doing it. Mom really felt deceived by me!

"She deserves better than that. She's a good person! She made all of us go out after supper to see the proof in the garden! Then, later, she cornered me and tried to get me to admit that I really did see something. I felt so sorry for her, all I could do to relieve her anxiety was to giggle mysteriously and tell her that I have 'all kinds of powers that I don't talk about!' She was so relieved to know that I did see something, she gladly accepted the idea that I could do it, rather than think something invisible was walking around out there.

"You knew you upset her and you didn't even care!" I was really on a roll now. "It was all right this time, because it was just her word against mine. But had anyone else been out there with us, I could not have covered for you! Now, I'm trying to help both of us here, but if you're going to be that obvious, there is no way I can keep your presence a secret! You just think about it!" I turned on my heels and left with the same saucy flair Teluke had left the garden with.

For a good while afterwards, every time I went out to check on them, I was sent away. Each time, I always told them I loved them and left. I tried not to bother them, but every time I slacked off the visits, Zanna would prod me to get back out there, because they weren't going to be around very long.

Teluke's greetings were not very pleasant. "Go away! I can kill you!"

"Would you, really? How?" I asked.

"I would pick you up by the feet and hit you against a tree! That is what we do with people we don't like! You would have to come in here."

Heck, I didn't know what this was all about. I prefer minding my own business, especially when I am not welcome.

I began to think of Teluke as a grouchy old man. I didn't take undue "poop" from him or anyone, for that matter. But, if it was due, I accepted what came. I felt we should be on pretty equal turf by now, so it was becoming annoying that he remained so belligerent with me.

I snuck out into the field, again keeping my thoughts to myself, for a girl chat with Teleel.

"Hi, Sweetie. Are you there?" I inquired.

"Yes, I am here," came her melodious voice. She was always so pleasant to my telepathic ears.

"How is the baby doing?" I asked her.

"Oh, she is growing so fast! She is so much fun!" she said.

I was delighted to have a decent reception for a change. "Oh, honey. You are so blessed! Do you play with her a lot?"

"Yes! We play all the time!" she said.

I was burning to hold or at least see the little one! "Golly, I want one of my own to play with, but my husband doesn't want one yet, so we will wait."

"You mean you people have control over your bodies that way?" she asked with surprise.

"No," I said. "Not the way you are meaning, but we have several ways to keep from having babies. I'm on medicine right now..."

"Oh, I have heard of medicine for that," Teleel broke in.

I went on. "Another way is to have an operation. This is where they cut you open and fix you so you can't have babies."

"Oh, that sounds like it would hurt a lot!" Her sincerity was always so touching. I couldn't help but feel close to her.

"No, they put you to sleep and you don't feel it. Does your mate play with her, too?" I asked her.

"Yes. My mate is a good father," she said softly.

Having touched him with our thoughts, Teluke felt it and realized we were conversing. I heard him ask her softly, "What are you doing talking to her?" Then his thoughts blasted upon me.

"What are you doing talking to my wife? Don't you ever speak to her again!"

I didn't like this intrusion and came back at him in an exasperated voice, "Go awaaaay! I'm not talking to you, old man! I came here to talk with Taleel!

"Who are you to say who she can speak with? Why don't you ask her if she wants to talk to me! She has a bright mind. She can think for herself!"

I heard her softly agree with me. I continued, "She's a lot smarter than you give her credit for. She can talk to who ever she wants to. She's not a slave. You don't own her!" Again, I heard her softly agree.

Telepathically, I could see him glance at her in surprise, then be bellowed, "If you ever speak to her again, I will kill her! I've already had to hit her once! She is acting more like you all the time!"

I was enraged! "You hit her? Kill her?" I yelled. "Don't you love her?"

"Yes," he answered, "I love her, but I would kill her before letting you get near hear! I hate you!"

I felt Teleel's alarm at this new realization of her mate's personality. I verbally flew back in his face. "That's not any kind of love that I know of! To kill someone to protect them? And then what are you going to do after that? Kill the baby?" I asked.

I felt the horror in both of them at this idea. Teluke was silent a moment, and I knew he was looking at the child. In a broken voice, he resigned his heart to the child and said, "No, I won't kill the baby."

I was still infuriated. "Oh, that's great! You are going to let the baby starve to death! You have no milk to feed her."

Teluke came back to life with fire. "I can feed the baby! She won't starve! I know how to take care of her! I hate you!"

I wanted to vomit at this whole obscenity. I told him he was disgusting, and I left. His whole attitude was more than disgusting to me. In some deep recess of my soul, I knew his people. They are extremely good, pure beings. Just their being on the earth helps hold the earth's vibrations on a level of non-destruction, counter-balancing all that the dominant race tries to do in its civilized ways.

But, every once in a while, you get one of these tyrants. I knew at one time, long ago, how to handle them. You just don't accept this bullying.

Before too long, I went back out into the field and sat down just within the force field. I wasn't thinking at Teluke, I was just thinking my own private thoughts as loudly as I could. He was his usual pompous self when he spoke to me, saying I was too close and to move further down the pasture.

I got up and moved down, but he said that wasn't far enough. So, I moved a nice piece further and sat down. He said it was still too close. The force field that keeps the horses from the woods was moving down the field as swiftly as I was. I was a bit dizzy and confused before I realized he had moved me two thirds of the way towards the barn! I got up and marched myself right back from where I started.

"Look!" I said matter-of-factly, "Who do you think you are? I can sit out here and think anywhere I want to! You just come in here and plant yourself on someone's land and claim it for your own! We were here first. If you aren't happy with what you have, you move!"

He shot back at me, "We were here first!"

"You were not! We were!" Was he out of his mind?

"Yes, we were! We were here first!" he insisted.

I was getting annoyed. "You were not!"

"Yes we were! My people were here long before you people were made!"

He seemed quite confident with his information.

I was just realizing what he was speaking about. "Your People? I'm not talking about whose people were here first! I don't even care! I'm talking about you and me! You planted yourself on a farm after we had been living on it for years. We were here first."

He was plenty mad and said, "Well, I'm taking over now!" He moved the force field. The birds in the front yard flew out of the trees. "Now, I claim the whole place! I'm taking back just part of what you people took from us long ago! It's mine now. Get off my land!"

I was mad as heck, and very frustrated. I clearly saw that he had moved the force field to claim the whole farm. Pretty impressive! It looked like an iridescent soap bubble enclosing the farm.

"Who do you think you are?" I protested. "You can't just come in here and take over!"

"I just did! Get off my land." he bellowed.

I refused to let him bully me this way. It was clear he had taken over, but I still had my free will. He wasn't going to live peacefully this way! I laid back in the grass and relaxed and daydreamed until he dropped the force field to its original place. Then I said to him, "You are welcome to use the woods and claim this portion of the pasture. But I will sit and think any where I please. You need to know the rules!" I went on and apologized for being a pest. "I don't like botherin' you all the time. I really don't! But, every time I try to leave you alone, the Star People tell me to get back out here."

"How do you know about the Star People?" he cried out. "Who told you about them?" He was thoroughly shocked, as though someone had infiltrated his family's secrets. "Our people are the only ones who know about them! You tell me who told you about them!" he demanded.

Trying to act casual, I replied, "The Star People, themselves."

"You are lying! They don't have anything to do with you people," he insisted. "You are not good enough! You tell me who told you and I will find him and kill him! It must be one of my people who told you, and I can't believe this. But, I will find him and kill him! You tell me who it is so I can kill him!"

I was getting tired. "I am not lying. I told you I am not like everybody else. The Star People told me. Ask them! Ask your wife!"

"Ask my wi..." Psychically, I saw him shoot a glance at her in shock. "What does she have to do with this?" I could feel his horror in thinking his mate was the traitor and he might have to kill her.

I continued. "The Star People have been working with me and my sisters all our lives. It is true, most people aren't accepted by them. But we are vibrationally different from everybody else. Your wife and I are old friends. We met on the ship when we were little children."

"That's a lie," he shouted. I told him to ask her.

I heard him pleading to her, "Is this true?" But he had so successfully shielded her from me I could not detect her thoughts anymore.

Teluke said he hated me and to go away. He said he had a lot to think about. I told him I loved them and left the field.

It was true. Zanna had taken me into the brilliant interior of the ship when I was the size of a six or seven year old. She had told me she had someone very special she wanted me to meet. I was left alone in the room, and soon Zanna escorted in the strangest little creature I had ever seen! A pretty little girl covered with silky dark hair! She stood a bit taller than I and we both gawked at each other. I realized that I must look as naked to her without hair as she looked over-dressed to me in her coat of hair, even though quite the opposite was true.

She stood there, heavily muscled, but with definite femininity emanating from her. She was barefoot and her feet were broad and looked worthy of good use. I too was barefoot, but in my pajamas I must have looked quite the waif. Shyly we both smiled reserved grins as Zanna explained that we would both be having children at approximately the same age (our children are about five years apart).

Zanna left us alone for a moment and I experienced a moment of embarrassment for the girl's nakedness. The girl beat me to the subject and asked what I had on my body. I told her they were my pajamas and asked if they had taken her clothes away from her and whether she was embarrassed walking around naked. Her response was one of surprise that such a thing would even occur to someone. She said I looked funny in my clothes and suddenly I felt funny in them.

# CHAPTER SIX

*The Power of One*

"...the smell of Power perks the ear

the voices of the tree

all darkened by the hand of God

with light hearts quick to flee..."

I TRIED TO GIVE THE SASQUATCH a rest from me. I really did. I knew I had dealt Teluke a big blow exposing the fact that some of my people do interact with the beloved Star People. He had a great deal to reconsider now. I didn't like bothering them at all anyway. I knew I wasn't wanted out there and that is no fun. He was such a tyrant all the time. He certainly had a beautiful, kind side to him, but since my two accidental blunders, I just never got to see that side of him anymore.

One afternoon, I was upstairs rattling around in my room when Zanna confronted me.

"It's almost time to capture your ally," she reported to me.

Switching over to the Second Attention, I automatically conversed with her.

"My What? I don't understand."

"Teluke! He is your ally. Do you know what that is?" she asked me.

"I guess it's a friend. Why do I need to capture him? He should remain free!" I didn't follow her train of thought.

She explained, "An ally is a friend, this is true. But it is much more! You must challenge him to do battle with you. If you win, you both serve to gain from it. If you lose, you both stay at the spiritual level you are now. If you win, he must help you in your life and you must teach him all you can. You are a medicine woman. You would be good anyway, but if you capture your ally you have his power working with you also! He must serve you."

I was in shock! All that "If you win" stuff didn't appeal to my sense of well-being at all! Zanna had a good sales pitch with all the positive sides to winning, but I noticed that she didn't have that much to say about losing!

"I don't like all this "if" you win stuff. Let's talk about if I lose! Heck! He's gonna kill me! There is no way I could win against a male Sasquatch or over a woman of his kind! I'm not gonna fight him! I don't stand a chance!" I fumbled around in a drawer.

Zanna was working on me. "I will be helping you. We want you to win!" (Well, that was reassuring. So did I!) She went on, "I will tell you what to do. Actually you stand a good chance of winning! If you didn't, we wouldn't have you do it! You have done well so far, but you stand to go much further in your growth if you do this!"

"I do?" That was the clincher, right there. She knew my heart. Long ago I had decided I would strive to be as good a person as I could possibly be. "I want to go as far as I can! Can I go all the way?" I was momentarily excited at the prospects of my spiritual maturity.

"Well, you will go very far up, but it would be difficult to go all the way in one lifetime," she explained.

It is difficult to explain the growth processes we endure in our earthly sojourns. She said something about there being a point that only certain entities achieve, which I would likely not attain in this short life.

Then my thoughts fell back to the reality of this world. A little girl fighting a male Sasquatch was out of the question! Sorta...did she say she would be helping me? Something about I 'stood a good chance'? I shelved the whole nonsense.

My daily trips out to the pasture were like slipping around in mud. Some days we did fairly well and on others we didn't hit it off.

I had attempted to find out as much about our two very different cultures as possible. In some ways they had a great deal to admire and in other ways, Teluke seemed to be at the same level that brings so much heartache into this world. I wanted to know about their position of morality.

I sat in the pasture talking with Teluke. "What would you do if your wife had a baby by another man?" It was an innocent enough question as far as I could see.

"What are you saying? Is there another man around here? I will kill him! Where is he?" He was on a tirade. I saw him dash to the borders of the woods and then turn in circles, searching the area. "There is no other man around here! What are you trying to do?"

I could feel Teleel's shock. She felt it was almost an accusation. "No! There is no other man around here! Your wife hasn't done this!" I tried to explain before things got out of hand.

"Then why would you bring it up! You people always try to start trouble!" he accused me.

I felt terrible. So often my innocent child side gets me in this position. "Please! I'm not trying to start trouble! I am wanting to know how your people look at situations compared to how my people look at things! I'm not trying to start trouble! I want to see if your people really are better than mine! What would your feelings be about this, and how would you feel about the child? Would you hate it or kill it or disown it?" I asked.

"Well, it would not be the baby's fault! I would keep it and love it," he said in a gentle voice.

"And what would your feelings be about your wife after that?" I asked.

"Well, it wouldn't be her fault either." He was calm and compassionate with me as he spoke.

"Then, let me ask you this. Would you feel differently if she allowed this to happen?" I needed to probe his feelings to see just how they are different than our society.

I sensed that he turned to look at her. "Well, I don't know. I would have to think about this. I don't want to talk about this any more."

Somehow, I felt as if I withdrew into a tipi that sat invisibly in the field with me. "Well, I have to say that you seem to be a little better than my people in this case. In my world, men often shun babies they do not father themselves. I am glad your heart is better."

One evening my best friend, Nan, my husband Byron and I were out riding in the paddock when we heard Teleel scream. I was working solely on the conscious level so I couldn't acknowledge to myself what it was. We all stopped and questioned the source. It sounded like a large feline, yet not like a cat, and it sounded like a woman's scream, yet not like a woman. We certainly had never heard anything like it before and pondered the thought that it came from the woods. We all knew the horses had stopped going up to the back to graze, and a couple of us were aware that the birds weren't back there anymore. None of us were brave enough to check it out.

The next day I asked Teluke if that was Teleel that screamed last night. He said 'yes'. I asked what was wrong. He looked at me and said they 'joined' last night.

"You mean you made love?" I wanted to be sure I understood him. He acknowledged this.

Expecting him to be like every other man I've met, I teased him about how good he must be at making love. He frowned in distaste. "You people aren't right!"

I realized my poor judgment and apologized. "I'm sorry! You are right! I don't like that attitude myself, but our men cause us to accept it. Most of our men are what we call 'womanizers', that judge their value upon sex. It is everything to them. I see you respect this the way I do, and I am glad to see that you hold this sacred with respect and dignity! I expected you to be like our men. The better results they have, the bigger they feel. I have never met a man who feels the way my heart does with respect for their mate in joining. I am honored to know you, Teluke!"

There were other days, though, when we did nothing more than throw verbal stones at each other. When he told me I looked stupid for the umpteenth time, I was ready for him.

"Well, I look more like the Star People than you do! I'm smaller and you have way too much hair! They don't have any hair at all! At least I mostly have mine on my head!"

"You don't look anything like the Star People! They are beautiful! You look stupid," he said.

"Well, you may think so, but they don't! They put us both here and you were the rough draft. They made a lot of improvements when they made us! They weren't satisfied with the results when they made you, so they made us then!" I wasn't sure how much of this was true, but it made for good ammunition. I so much wanted to get along, but I wasn't going to be anybody's rug, either.

Just when I thought I was doing all that I could to interact, Zanna came back into the picture as the bad penny.

"I guess you are not going to capture your ally. I am really sorry to hear that. You stood a good chance too!"

Oooooh, don't remind me! My soul seemed to moan. It wasn't a thought. It was a feeling, like throwing a report card away without looking at it, because you know it's a bad one. You hope no one sees it. But I knew myself. I knew if I stood to gain spiritual ground from this obscenity (and she did seem hopeful for my success), that I would toss caution to the wind.

I didn't understand why it seemed so important to do it now, though! I had the whole summer to put it off!

But she explained, "Well, it has to be done now if you are going to win. Your chances are better if you do it now. It is almost too late, already!"

I asked her to explain this, and without her having the exact words we use, I understood it had to do with the stars' positions and the energy.

"What do I have to do?" I asked, resigning myself to the situation. I had decided to do my best and give it all I had. I just had to ignore how the odds looked to me. Zanna had faith in me that I didn't have. That was enough.

"You must not wear your clothes. You must purify yourself, and have a power," Zanna instructed. I didn't know what I was doing. It sounded good, though.

"How do I purify myself?" was to me the most logical thing to ask.

"With water," she replied. "but, don't use any chemicals after you purify yourself. Don't wear clothes or shoes then.""Zanna! I can't walk around naked! We have rules! The neighbors would have me hauled away!" I was worried now, that this might prevent me from going forward in my spiritual quest here. I would go naked and dare the whole neighborhood if it got me closer to the Creator somehow. But I had to find an alternative, if there was one.

"Well, wear skins then, as you once used to. But, don't wear those shoes. The bottoms aren't real."

Again, I was panicked momentarily. "Zanna! I gotta wear something on my feet! I can't outrun a Sasquatch barefoot in a hay field! I'll injure my feet!"

She seemed to have the utmost patience with me. She wasn't the least bit unnerved. "Then can you find shoes like you once wore, that are made of skin?"

Immediately, I knew I had what was called for. "Yes, I have that!"

"Good. You will need a feather tied in your hair, a shield, and a power object, a cane of some kind," she informed me.

I was ready to go to work! "Where do I start?"

"Well," she thought, "get your skins together first, I believe."

Once I decide to do something, it is whole hog or nothing. I was really anxious. My gears were in motion. I ran into the house and flew up the stairs to my room. Tearing through the closet, I was frantic to find anything to make a loincloth out of. I was freaking out! I couldn't find a thing! I ran back downstairs and asked Mom if there was any leather I could have to cut up. I needed a big piece!

Mom saw the urgency in me and looked until she found an old suede coat she had gotten at a garage sale. I thanked her and ran upstairs. It didn't take long to do, and I cut a strip to tie it with. I tried it on and found it suitable. Next, I dug out my knee-high lace-up moccasins and threw them on the bed. I found my leather vest that was fringed from the bust to the waist, and tried the whole thing on. It was decent. I didn't look as bad as I had thought I would. I asked Zanna for her opinion and she said it was fine. "Now you need to make a shield."

All this was totally foreign to my conscious person. Anything Native I had leaned towards in my life had been strictly instinctual. I had always loved Native Americans, and it was natural for me to collect medicine, as the Natives understand it, but I never knew it was medicine or power or anything other than normal for me. I had never even read about their shields, so this was especially new to me. I asked Zanna about it and she gave me a brief description to draw or paint it.

So, at first I put it on a piece of paper and she had me do it over. She had neglected to tell me that I would be taking it with me into the field. I got a piece of cardboard that just barely passed inspection because it was made from trees. She had me draw a circle and put myself in it, showing me winning the battle. I had to put an eagle in it, as well.

I refused to make it a bloody scene showing anybody hurt, so I just made Teluke itty-bitty, and myself large and having control of him with my hand. Zanna questioned me what it was and chuckled when I explained it. Next, I was instructed to put a thong on it so I could wear it and have my hands free.

"Now go and purify yourself. And remember not to use any chemicals on your body afterwards," she said.

Zanna never said how much time I had exactly, but I felt the need to keep hopping. After my bath, in my haste, I automatically sprayed my armpits with deodorant, when Zanna shouted at me! Horrified and feeling some invisible clock ticking away my chances, I had to suds up the washcloth and frantically try to erase my sin, wondering how contaminated I remained afterwards.

I went upstairs and put on the regalia. Zanna told me to braid my hair, which I did. I ran downstairs to where Mom was working in the kitchen. "Well, look at you! What are you up to?"

The family had somewhat gotten used to me being a bit strange these days. I just giggled and said, "Oh, just having fun! How do I look?"

Mom said I looked fine, then forbade me to leave the house! She was afraid the neighbors might see, but I excused myself and went on outside. I was covered and not indecent.

Zanna then told me I needed a feather to tie in my hair. I took the first one I found, a small house sparrow's wing feather. Zanna said it wouldn't do. It had to be bigger. I ran to the barn and found a blue pigeon feather. Again, she said no. "Your people used to use one of the meat eaters," she explained.

Now, I'm not in the habit of thinking of birds as being carnivorous. I think of sweet little seed eaters like canaries and parakeets. Calling birds 'meat eaters' brought to mind visions of Pterodactyl or Pteranodon, before she clarified herself. "You would call it a 'bird of prey'. One of the large birds, a hawk or eagle, but **not** an owl."

Oh, Lord! When was the last time I had even seen a hawk? "I don't know if I can find one soon, Zanna! I will have to look for days! Do I have time?" I was willing, but Zanna said, "No, there isn't time. We only have this afternoon." Then, after thinking a moment, she said, "Then you must use the biggest one you can find. A white one!"

Great. I was going to have to face a male Sasquatch with improvised power, one that I picked out of pigeon shit. I didn't feel very lucky at that moment. I didn't feel like my chances were as good as Zanna had spoken of either. But, either the white feather I found pleased her, or she let me believe it was just the ticket in order to rekindle my shriveling spirits. She had me tie it into my braid and then set me off to get some wood.

I found a piece of board, not knowing what was needed, and was chastised. She directed me to the trees in the yard. Again, I picked up the first measly twig I came across and she said I needed a big one. "One of the larger arms of the tree."

"Larger arms? Like a limb?" Zanna seemed to begin to be a bit exasperated and was starting to see just how little I really understood what I was doing. She directed my eyes, by looking through them, to a nice curvy branch on the ground which was about an inch thick and three feet long. I asked if I should peel it, but she said not to.

I asked what I was supposed to do with it, because I sure wasn't going to hit him with it or poke him!

Zanna told me that I just needed to carry it. "But do **not** let it leave your hands for **any** reason! And do not go into the woods! Make him come out to you into the pasture. The pasture is your battle ground. That is where your power is!" I was ready! I marched out into the hay field wondering in what condition the family would find me. An arm here, a leg there, an empty chest cavity ...

It was a gorgeous day! I was clean, strong, confident. I didn't know what the hell I was doing, but I felt good as my pigeon feather waved in the breeze.

As I walked through the pasture up to the force field, I couldn't take myself seriously. I asked Zanna what I should do. She said to announce myself.

"Old man! I am here!" What a riot, I thought. Even I wouldn't be scared of me if I was looking out from the woods. This has got to be a joke, right?

Teluke was just as disdainful as ever. "Go away."

"I am here to challenge you to do battle!" I said to him.

He retorted, "I won't fight a female. It would waste my time. I could kill even one of your best males. You are no match for me. Go away!"

"No! You will come out and face me," I challenged him. He became momentarily distracted by my attire.

"What do you have on your body?"

"It is my battle regalia," I explained.

He commented, "It looks better than your other clothes. What is that in your hair?"

"It is a feather," I said.

Again he was still side-tracked. His tone changed to a more than casual one. "What is it for, and what is in your hands?"

I felt I had my foot in the door, now. "They are for power! I have come to fight you!"

"Go away! I will not waste my time with a female!"

Them's fightin' words! I couldn't help but feel some insecurity in his voice when I spoke about my power objects. Something that said to me that within himself, he saw this was more serious than he let on.

I asked Zanna what I was to do now.

"Aggravate him. Get him mad," she told me.

My mind turned immediately to my brother, the greatest antagonist in the world. He loves nothing more than to 'rattle someone's cage'. I was reminded of one of his favorite lines from an old Bugs Bunny cartoon.

"Old man!" I paused to be sure I had his attention. "Your Mother wears army boots!" I laughed to myself at the stupidity of this old trick. It is so old it doesn't even work anymore in our society. Zanna questioned me. I chuckled, knowing what it was going to do to him. I toed the grass, grinning at my foot while I waited for his response.

"What's that?" he snapped.

I telepathed a picture of a Sasquatch with hanging breasts, in army boots. It was ridiculous and I laughed inside. He was outraged!

"No, she doesn't!" he screamed at me.

"Yes, she does! Greeaat big ones, too!" I then ballooned the boots in the picture to be as long as she was tall! I felt as mean as my brother when he used to pick on us littler guys, and give us 'Indian sunburns'. I was thoroughly delighted with myself!

That got Teluke furious! "She does not! That's not my Mother! You don't know my Mother! Don't you ever speak about my Mother again, or I will kill you! I mean this! I have always wanted to kill one of your people!"

Zanna said to let him cool down. "It would be too easy for him to -- your people say, 'strike while the iron is hot'. He would come out right now and do it and it would all be over."

"What do I do now, then?" I asked her in bewilderment.

"Go to your power spot and sit down," she instructed.

"Power spot? What power spot?" I had no idea what she was talking about.

"You know! Your place of Power!" She seemed frustrated.

"Where is that? I don't understand." And I didn't.

"Where you always sit," Zanna explained.

Oohhh! I always knew it felt good there, but I had no idea it had anything to do with my power. I always chose a slight rise in the ground there in the field when I would come out here to visit. It was just my instincts for naturally finding my medicine.

She said to lie down and talk to him.

I lay down in the tall grass, lying parallel to the back fence. I laid my stick down and got comfortable.

**"Pick it up! Pick it up!** Pick up your stick and don't let it leave your hands again!" Zanna snapped at me for the first time. The urgency in her voice made me break out into a sweat and reminded me that this was not a game, though I was having a ball, so far.

I grabbed the stick immediately, feeling rather stupid. Somewhere, while the stick had been out of my hands, I felt a sly grin emanate from the woods, as though Teluke was keenly aware of my mistake. Shoot, I was having a hard time being serious. I didn't know what the hell it was all about, or what I was doing out there in the first place! But Zanna's urgency got my attention back on track. I began talking.

"I know you hate me. But I love you! You really break my heart. You know that?" It was a good place to start, anyway. I went on, "I have always believed deep in my soul, that your people were good, pure beings. I always felt that they were here helping with the same job I was doing. Trying to make this world a better place! I felt that just your people being here was raising the vibrations that hold this world together. I was counting on your people's pureness to help lift the world out of darkness! But, I see I was wrong."

Zanna told me to pour myself into it. She told me to feel deeply and cry, for power.

I meant every word of it. I was beginning to reach down into the recesses of my soul. What I felt brought out waves of despair. My love for the planet and all good things was intense, and my fear for it racked me with pain.

"But, I see that you are no better than my own people, hating and wanting to kill innocents that mean you no harm." I wept, a totally broken child, without any hope left. I had never felt this level of complete despair or felt so totally alone before. I saw my path before me, and it was indeed grim. My chest was hurting and I had a rock in my throat that I couldn't get rid of with my tears.

"God is going to come back here soon to check out His creation. If He doesn't find any love or goodness here, He will destroy it!" I felt Teluke agree with me. He seemed surprised that I knew of this.

I continued. "I was relying on your peoples' help to tip the scales of pureness and love. I see now that it is just up to me! I am all that is left, if the world is going to be spared! It's up to me alone now to show the Creator there is still love here so He won't destroy it!" I literally was carrying the weight of the whole world and it was more than I could bear.

I was completely shattered as I lay on my back, sobbing.

"I can't go on living in a world without any love! If you are an example of your people, I don't want to be here any more!"

Zanna spoke up and said not to soften him too much. She said to reel him in now. Take away his power. I had forgotten what we were doing, and had become totally absorbed into my sad plot in life.

"What do I do?" I asked her telepathically up on the ship.

"Tell him he's dying."

"Dying? I don't understand." I didn't know what to do with that.

"Then let me talk for you." There seemed to be no time to stall. I agreed to turn over the reins to her.

I stumbled along the first few words with her, thinking that I was supposed to help in some way. My words echoed hers as I tried to repeat simultaneously what she was saying.

"What are you doing?" she said startled. She warned me that he could hear me, and told me not to help her. She told me to let her do it all and not to try to talk.

"Who are you talking to? I thought I heard somebody else," he asked me.

Zanna replied for me, "Do you see anyone else out here? Old man! Did you hear me, **Old Man?**"

"Stop calling me that! I'm not old!" he exclaimed.

"I'm sorry you are dying." I waited for his reaction to this, totally amused and snickering to myself

"Dying? I am not dying." It was almost a question, as if he thought I knew something he did not. "Go away!" He seemed desperate to get rid of me, like a tormenting fly on a sandwich.

"Yes, you are dying! You are **old** and **dying**." She continued, "You are so old you are almost on your death bed!" This was hilarious to me. I could telepathically feel what he was going through, and it seemed a great deal of confusion confronted him. He took stock of himself.

"I am not! I'm not much older than you are!"

"Yes." She used a sing-song voice, light, airy and certain. "You are at death's door. You are a dying man and that is what makes you so bitter and angry. You are wasting away your life force right now, with all of your hatred. You hate me because I am so young and healthy and beautiful, and I have my whole life ahead of me, while you are dying!" I waved my arm in grandeur.

Teluke was getting pretty steamed again. I couldn't help feel that part of it was because of saying I was so beautiful, when we both knew how he felt about my looks.

I could feel his loathing at my peskiness. Zanna turned it back over to me, then.

"Go away! I hate you!" He could almost not stand to hear me by now.

"I know you hate me! But I love you! I believe in love! I can love you more than you can hate me, and I will prove how much I love you! I will give you something you have always wanted!"

"How do you know what I have always wanted?" he asked with disgust at my audacity.

"Because you told me," I responded.

"What's that?" He seemed curious now.

"I will give you one of my people to kill!"

This caught him completely off guard. "You will?"

I could almost see him wringing his hands! He accepted the idea immediately.

"Who?" he asked.

"Me!" I shot back.

"Go away! You would be too easy to kill. Go, before I take you up on this! I really want to kill you!"

"I'm not afraid to die! It is a good day to die!" I always loved that line. It was appropriate, too. "Come on out here and pull my arms out of their sockets, and eat my face off if you think this will

81

make you better than my people! I don't want to live any more anyway! You might as well go ahead and kill me. You are doing it anyway, a little at a time, with all of your hatred!"

He was about to cross the line. "I mean it. I will kill you," Teluke warned.

"I mean it, too!" I responded. "Come on out and kill me! I won't even defend myself. I have no weapons! Come on out here and get it over with!"

"I am coming," he warned, as if to give me a chance to change my mind. I looked down between my feet as I lay there and saw he had leaped over the fence and was standing there waiting to see my reaction.

"Yep," I thought to myself. "He's coming. You sure you want to go through with this?" (It's always a good idea to introspect before serious decisions.) I introspected. Yes! It was true. I didn't want to be here if his people were not guarding the earth as I knew them to be. I had nothing to live for! I couldn't carry the world alone. I didn't want to be the only one with real love left here, as I felt at that moment. I waved him on.

He was at my feet like lightning. "Get up!" he bellowed. "We don't kill things that are just lying there like you people do!"

"Oh? And just how do you people **kill**?" I exaggerated the word to get my point across.

He stumbled on his words at first then said, "We let them have a chance! Get up and run down the pasture and I will chase you and kill you!"

I was disgusted. "That's no chance! That is cruel! Giving someone hope when there is none! No," I went on in a sing-song voice of my own now, "I will lie here, thank you."

Teluke kicked me on my left thigh with a thud and ordered me up. I was getting mad. He hurt me!

"No, now! This is my dying moment and I get to choose how I want to die! Don't you know the rules? I don't want to hit the ground when I die. So, I will be down here when you kill me!" I laid there with my eyes closed trying to stay relaxed. "Kill me where I am!"

He kicked me again. This was going to be painful in a minute and I didn't want to stick around to feel it. Zanna told me to get out of there, now!

My astral body swiftly leaked out my navel and I swirled myself around his ankles and was behind him. I had hoped he had not noticed me. He kicked my arm with a blow that could have broken something. The body flopped lifeless. He put his foot on her chest and sprang it a few times. I observed quietly. She didn't need this and I knew that I had better intervene. I hauled back and kicked him in the ass with my astral foot. To my amazement, it went on through him, feeling like warm pudding to my leg. Trying to pull my foot up to the calf back out was like a fly sticking to chewing gum. It took a great deal of force and momentum. Zanna seemed to have grabbed me to help pull me back. When my foot freed, Zanna was frightened for me and told me explicitly not to touch him anymore! She said I could get trapped inside with him.

"Wouldn't that be wonderful," I thought, "being stuck inside the same body with a tyrant? What a nightmare!"

He didn't feel it anyway, so I had to act fast to distract him. I zoomed up to his ear and shouted, "I'm not in there!"

He was shocked and surprised and swung around, flinging his fist out. I zipped just as swiftly around him again. "Here I am! Over here!" I announced.

He spun around again and swung. I stayed behind him taunting him. Teluke was almost hysterical. His eyes were wide and filled with terror. I laughed at him and buzzed his head a few times like a mad hornet.

"You think you are so special because you can do a few tricks with your body! But I have my own power! It is called love." I said.

He was hysterical, spinning and swinging at the air. I spun faster and faster about his head until I became a halo of white light about his head and between us connected the common bond of the Creator. It was a complete circle. The Sacred Medicine Wheel of life that connects all things and from which he saw his own reflection of his own goodness, in my halo. When the connection was completed, he squeaked out a yell of recognition.

In exasperation, he stopped and stood there for just an instant, then flagged his arm at me in resignation and turned and walked away. The brawny man was defeated.

I eased back down into my body wondering if anything was broken. Was it a dream? Oooooh, no. I felt like I had been beaten with a board! I twisted my wrists and arms and stretched my legs. Nothing was broken.

"Hey! My arms and legs are still attached," I called out to him. "I still have my face! Where are you going? Don't you want to kill me anymore?"

# CHAPTER SEVEN

## Emerging Positions

"...but caught the eye of innocent

in swirling spires the mind was sent

as dust upon the doily blew..."

T HE NEXT DAY I STAYED up at the house. It was hot and I had put on as little as was decent. I was stiff, but it was Mom that noticed my bruises on my left arm and leg. I was pleased about them, but I had no explanation for them, to speak of. To me they were like badges of honor, not for having been abused, but for the very real act of challenging a male Sasquatch and winning.

Later in the week I caught sight of a piece of barn wood laying in the shed row of the barn that had a hole in it. Each time I passed it I would notice it. My thoughts were that it should be good for something, but I continued to leave it lie and went on with my chores. It was Zanna trying to inspire me, but I didn't catch the hint.

Later that day I heard a noise that was music to my soul. It felt like a sudden starvation for long ago loved ones. A loud, low whirring that seemed to pulsate, striking me at the very core with a kind of music that tugged at my spirit!

I ran out of the barn immediately, looking for its source. I saw my sister-in-law with one hand on her knee whirling something on a rope over her head. It was the source of this sound I loved. I ran over to her and asked her if I could try it. She said yes, and showed me the details. It was that piece of barn siding with the hole in it, put on a thong. I let it fly around and around over my head just long enough to catch the gist of it and asked her if it would be all right if I borrowed it for a few minutes. She said yes, that she was through with it now anyway.

I ran out into the pasture and whirled it around and around, bringing forth that mesmerizing tone pulsing, whirring.... I could get lost in the sound.

Teluke ran out to me instantly, panic stricken. "What is wrong? Why did you call me?" His voice trailed off when he saw it was just me.

"I didn't call you," I assured him. I was surprised to see him run out to me. "Nothing is wrong. Why?"

"Yes, you did! That thing in your hands called me!" He was getting more peeved at me every second.

"You don't even know what you are doing! You people are so stupid!" The scowl on his face was of utter contempt for bothering him.

I felt about two feet tall. "I'm sorry! We found this and were playing with it. I didn't know what it was." I hated having to admit to him that I really didn't know what I was doing.

"Well, you people should learn to leave things alone if you don't know what it is! The next time you see something you don't know about, leave it alone!"

I apologized and went back in the house. I realized the seriousness of the thing my sister-in-law had made and asked her if I could have it, partly because I felt it belonged to me on a deeper level, and largely because I knew she would get in trouble with it.

She said that it belonged to her and she wanted to play with it. I told her that it was not a toy and that she should not play with it at all, but at the same time, I realized it didn't seem that she was going to listen to me.

Later on, we heard her screaming outside and she came running into the house crying and all upset. Mom was right there for her and was appalled when she told her that a naked man attacked her.

Mom wanted to call the police, but sis reported he was invisible and was gone now. Mom hollered, "Invisible?"

Sis stormed past me and threw the Bull Roarer at me. "Here! You can have the dumb thing! I don't want it any more!

Today, I understand that what was concocted, with Zanna's help, was a Bull Roarer. I have never seen an authentic one, but have recreated the one that we used that day. I am told by others who have seen them, that it is made correctly. Its time of use was about upon me.

At the end of the week I went home to visit my own family. I can't be sure whether the conversation was telepathic or verbal, but things were such that I could easily talk verbally with them about it and it would have been accepted in a humorous mood.

I recall my folks asking me what all I had been up to and I very light heartedly said, "Ooooh, I fought a male Sasquatch this week." I knew they would not necessarily believe me, so I could truthfully say something like that. This was very typical of me to have something outstanding to speak about. I have always had incredible experiences like this, and though my family was open to such things, they still preferred to think I just had a wild imagination than to fully accept that I am telling the truth about these things.

Naturally, they laughed, so I continued. "I won, too! I told him his mother wears army boots!" They thought it was hilarious and the subject was dropped. It gave me just the vent I needed to air the pressure of my secret and keep it bearable for me.

The following week after the battle, I called Teluke out into the pasture to meet with me. I had left him alone because I felt he had more healing to do than I did. Teluke responded and came out.

As he approached, he said, "I don't want to, but the Star People said that I had to do what ever you want me to do. What do you want me to do?" His tone was disgusted, like he expected me to enslave him with things that would violate him.

"I don't want anything from you. All I want is for you to learn to trust that I won't hurt you. I just want you to be a friend. That's all!" That was true. I certainly would take no joy in having my way with anyone if it was against their will. He was disbelieving as his long strides brought him closer.

"You don't even want my powers? You could be...very big among your people!" My reasoning astounded him.

My head swam with the thought of healing people. What a wonderful thing this would be. But, then I saw the problems. People disbelieving in a 22 year old, a girl-wonder, a Christ prodigy, others flocking to my house. My life would be turned upside down and I would never be the same. Zanna was also cautioning me. What ego trips would I go through because I wasn't mature enough to handle such a gift? No thanks.

"I don't want anything from you except your friendship. You have your family to raise and one day I will have mine. Maybe someday, after we are through with our jobs with family, then I will take you up on healing people and your power. All I want from you right now is to try to trust that I only want your friendship. I want you to be my friend!"

Teluke came within five or six feet of me, meeting me out in the pasture for the first time other than the battle. He was quite invisible to my eyes, yet very physical. He smashed down the hay with each step. It was my Second Attention that allowed me to view him. He wasn't a huge Sasquatch, but as a man he was enormous.

"I thought you people were supposed to be huge! You're short!" I stated. He was only the size of a tall man, possibly 6 1/2 feet tall. I hadn't had the opportunity to really examine him before

"I am one of the smaller ones. Some of my people are very big!" He telepathed the image of a huge 15 foot Sasquatch to me. I was impressed! We stood there analyzing each other. He told me again that I looked stupid.

"Oh, yeah! Well, I can look right up into your nostrils! Don't tell me I look stupid, while I look up your nose," I defended myself. Zanna was watching over the situation from the ship, and I heard her chuckle.

I stood there a moment in awe. "Actually, I think you are beautiful," I said softly.

As I studied his eyes, a deep rumble began to emanate from his throat. How 'gorilla' he looked! Yet in the image of man! His eyes were very human. It was like a man in a gorilla's body! His head was pointy on top with the sagittal crest of the Great Apes, and his face was very gorilla-like, except around the eyes. His nose was more than a gorilla has, but less than we have. His mouth was wide and ape-like, yet had a human quality about it.

I continued to study his eyes, as the rumble in his throat got louder. I was smiling in admiration of his beauty, but he continued to growl louder and his lips began to curl. The realization hit me that people can't growl like this, and he snarled louder at my thought, like a dog just before it bites. I grew horribly frightened!

"What's wrong?" I literally felt like I had a tiger by the tail, or in any case, a beast!

"I don't like you," he snarled.

"Why? I love you!" I looked deep into his eyes for an answer, when I was attacked in a loud roaring snarl! I threw my hands over my face and turned aside.

"What did I **do**? I didn't do anything!"

But he snapped back at me, "You look me in the eyes and I don't like it!"

"Well of course I do! That's how I was raised! My people believe that if you are honest, you aren't afraid to look others in the eye. They believe that the people who don't look you in the eye have something to hide! I am showing you I am honest by allowing you to look me in the eye and see my soul! We say 'the eyes are the window of the soul'!"

Listening, he scrunched up his face and appeared to reach way down into my eyeball to see my soul.

"You look _me_ in the eye! If it disturbs you, you can look away, too, ya know," I told him.

It's a crazy cultural practice we have chosen, because one gives away power in eye contact. Respect for others allows privacy. Indigenous people all over the world protect their power and privacy by avoiding eye contact as well as keeping one's name private.

I went on. "Why don't you like it? What is it that you think I am saying to you? That I am a threat?" I tried to keep my eyes off of his, but my upbringing was instinctive by that age and he growled and snarled every time my eyes crossed his.

"My people just don't like it!" He charged me again as we stood there.

"I am trying to not look at you. Can I look at your body?" I was swimming for the rules.

"Yes," he said.

I noticed that in between snarls his tone returned to a pleasant, very neutral tone. There was no lingering anger, no residue of bad feelings to work through. When the attack was over, it was over. That's it. There seemed to be nothing to forgive.

"Can I look at your face?" I was needing to know all the borders. I wanted all my privileges and wanted to know just where the line was drawn. I was desirous to please him and learn to get along. I certainly didn't mind learning the appropriate customs of his people.

"Yes, you may look at my face," he said calmly.

I wasn't familiar with people having this custom then, but I was familiar with animals. Some animals do not like eye contact with humans, either. So I understood, at least in part.

He heard my thoughts compare him to an animal and snarled in disgust. "I am not an animal!"

I promptly acknowledged this and apologized. As we tried to continue this meeting, we were both interested in our differences. I had him turn his head so I could see his ears. They were smaller than ours, and if memory serves me correctly, they were rather fuzzy.

He had me pull my hair back to expose my ears to him. He asked me about my earrings. I asked if I could see his teeth and he parted his lips. They were, naturally, larger than mine, but very pretty. He did have slightly larger canines than ours are proportionally. I asked him to open his mouth, which he did.

Beautiful white teeth for any human! No cavities or grime. Pure white healthy teeth. His tongue was large, but so was everything about him. I dreaded the next move. I had to expose my maw with all its fillings and stuff. Naturally, I had a lot of explaining to do. I told him about our heavily sugared diets.

I had him show me his hand. Broad, squat and large, nails were naturally worn, but they were clean. The backs were covered with nice thick hair right down the fingers, thinning out only toward the ends.

He asked to see mine. They looked frail compared to his, and were slender, long fingered and the nails were long. He asked in curious surprise about my long nails. I told him we like them to be long because it makes women look more feminine. I had to explain this further. Later on he brought Teleel up to show her my nails and asked her to try to let hers grow. But it didn't turn out too successfully and she gave up. I really felt bad for her that he would compare her to me in any way, but she didn't seem to mind.

We were both genuinely curious about each other. He could be so pleasant when he wanted to be. I relished these moments! I loved every instant of contact when he was civil with me. Every nuance about the situation was extraordinary. His features, his animal likeness, his scent, his massive size, all his unique traits, not to mention his rarity, his invisibility, his connection to the Star

People. The opportunity alone to be so honored as to interact with the subject of numerous mysteries that intellects everywhere were seeking high and low for! I had it all right there before me, person to person! He was mine!

I found the urge beyond my control to keep my eyes from wandering back to his, and bringing on continual attacks if I tried to believe I could look at his face and not look at them. I continued to gravely apologize and asked that he have patience with me, as I tried to retrain myself to his custom. However, it was an impossible request for me and I at last told him, "I guess I am just going to have to not allow myself to look at your face! I can't seem to help myself and I don't mean to insult you this way." For a long time after that, I kept bent over to force my eyes to obey. I would not even allow myself to look above the waist at him because I desperately wanted to oblige him and make him a friend.

He seemed to see my consternation and genuine attitude and withheld any hard feelings about my slip-ups, even though he continued to reprimand me with a snarling attack for a good while. At times he would go so far as to realize I had forgotten and would say in frustration, "Don't **look** at me!" It was reassuring to me that he was understanding of my cultural training. It proved intelligence and was very human. I heard his private thoughts one day when I was just so happy to be getting along.

"She's forgotten."

I looked up into his eyes and asked, "Forgotten what?", smiling at my new friend.

"You are looking at me!'

I chastised myself up one side and down the other. "I am so sorry! Please forgive me! I didn't mean to. Oh, Lord! Please forgive me! You are absolutely right! I totally forgot. I'll try harder. I didn't mean to! I feel so bad. Please forgive me!" I was panicked that this would backslide our relationship. I had so freely accepted this new friendship that I had made another error, which I could not afford at this late date. We seemed to have come so far!

"Well, that's okay. You don't have to feel bad, just don't do it anymore," he told me patiently.

As long as I was trying hard to work on it, he kept a light air about it, if we were alone and not with his family. He never fully stopped the attacks all together, to keep me in check, but they were for different reasons. It was never malice because I could see it wasn't part of his light. He didn't hold malice. It was at times felt, but it was gone as quickly as it appeared and it left no residue of darkness in him as it does with us when we linger with it in our hearts, having to work through it.

# CHAPTER EIGHT

## A Cautious Truce

"...whose voice is but the soft sweet

flutter of a moths wings calling my name out

in such a whisper as to cause my soul to quiver..."

O N THAT FIRST MEETING IN the field after the battle, we
continued our inspection of each other on a more obscure
basis from then on. His hair was roughly three and a half inches
long in most places, with it longer down the back of his head and
neck. When he raised what would be known as 'hackles', he looked
top heavy and one might mistake it for a mane.

The hair remained long on the full back of his hand and grew
sparse and just a bit shorter between the first and second knuckle.
His feet were broad but human in size, having hair covering about
half of the tops of them and then tapering off. I recall that he
had only three decent size toes which I found ugly at first, and
embarrassingly often had mud between them. But this is to be
expected when one goes barefoot constantly.

Teluke's arms were stocky and well muscled. He was broad
chested and well muscled in the hips and calves, having the square
kind of calves I find unappealing on men. However, he had a nice
plumpness about him and not a hard muscled body like a body
builder has.

He asked me about my jewelry and said his people are beautiful
enough, so they didn't have to hang things from their bodies.

"Would you let me see your hat?" he asked me with a challenging
expression.

Without hesitation, to continually show my trust of him, I
whipped it off and handed it to him. "Sure!"

He took it, but before examining it asked me, "You aren't afraid
to let me have it?"

"No," I began, "I trust that you will give it back. If you were to ruin it for me or take it, I can always get another one. I would rather have you for a friend than have a hat," I said trustingly.

"I think I will keep this hat," he said as he turned and walked away.

"Hey! Where are you going?" I called to him.

"You said I could have it," he retorted.

"No, I said I trusted you to give it back," I reminded him.

"You said you could always get another one," he reminded me. He stopped and looked at me.

"But I don't want another one! I like that one," I said in return. "The point is that I don't think you really want the hat! I think you are just being mean!" I was sad to think that he would be this way. I was so sick of people doing this kind of thing. Teluke seemed to loathe our people so at times that it just didn't fit that he would want to use something like a hat.

I meant what I said, and if he had accidentally ruined it or really liked it and wanted it for his own, I would have gladly given it to him. But this was just stinkiness!

"Oh, keep it!" I turned to leave and broke down crying from the hurting.

"Here, you can have it back. I don't want the stupid thing," he said as he approached me again.

When he thrust it forward, I wouldn't take it. "You haven't looked at it yet. You can try it on if you want to," I said swallowing back my tears. My hope was renewed.

He was surprised by me. He examined it a moment, then stuck it on top of his head. I was immediately embarrassed for him. His sagittal crest, the point on his head, caused the hat to be unstable and wobble around on its pinnacle. Telepathically I **felt** him internalize the strangeness of having something so foreign on his head. I could actually feel it as if it were on my own head for the very first time!

To stabilize it, he lifted his chin up. His sagittal crest forced the hat to sit way back behind his brow giving him an extremely greenhorn look that was appalling! His face was blank as he thought about it. Either he felt as ridiculous as he looked, or he telepathed from me my embarrassment for him.

He whipped it off his head and gave it back to me in a disgusted way. "Here! I don't need something on my head. It's stupid!"

When he saw I didn't laugh (I was just too embarrassed to), he asked me how he looked in it. I told him honestly that it didn't do him justice. I told him they make hats with taller tops though, that would fit him better. I was praying that he wouldn't want me to get him a ten-gallon hat.

"I wasn't going to keep it. I just wanted to see if you were lying to me," he said apologetically.

"Did I pass your stupid test?" I asked disgustedly.

"Yes." His tone was almost as if he wished I had not.

"You sound like you're sorry I did," I told him accusingly.

"I am. I don't want anything to do with you."

"How come you're always such an asshole? I'm trying to be your friend!" I wasn't really pleased with his ingredients so far.

"What's an asshole?" he asked me.

I telepathed his rear-end rather graphically.

"That's not all of me! Is that all you can see? There is more to me than that," he sputtered, confused and hurt.

"Well, that's the only side of you I ever get to see! The stinky side!"

He seemed to think about this a moment. "Well, You people say we smell bad to them."

"I'm not talking about your body odor. When somebody is being ornery, cantankerous, naughty on purpose, we say they just plain stink. We call them stinky! They are stinkers! You stink this way! So, the name is befitting. **Asshole.** That's the only part of yourself you show to me. I would very much like to get to see the rest of you sometime!"

He seemed to think about this and our mood changed. I asked him about his invisibility. "Where do you go when you are invisible, when I can't see you?" I clarified.

"We go to another ...," he searched for words. "It's like this place, but..."

I tried to help him. "Another world or dimension?"

"Yes, but it's ...". He scanned the area searching for something, then looked at the sun. "...like up there."

"You mean yellow?" I asked.

"Yes, but it's more ...". He was thinking.

I picked up telepathically a deeper yellow and looked for the color on my brown and yellow flannel shirt.

"Like this?" I asked, holding out a shirt square.

"Yes, something like that. You are good at this." He complimented me on my telepathy.

"Do you think you could take me in there with you if I held onto your hand?" I asked eagerly.

"I don't know. I don't know of any of your people that have ever tried it. It could kill you," he responded with concern.

I'm not afraid to die," I said. We both grinned. We reflected to the last time I had said that.

"Are you sure?" he asked me as he held his hand out to me. I stepped forwards and was about to take it when it occurred to me to introspect first before trying it.

"Well, just a minute. Let me check on something first. Let me think a moment," I corrected myself so he would not realize what I was about to do, in case he disapproved.

Somehow, either astrally or telepathically, I connected with Zanna on board the ship. "Teluke and I were talking about being invisible and he is willing to take me in there with him. We don't know if it will kill me or not. It is okay if I try it?" I asked.

Zanna's motherly overtures were comforting. She always knew about these things concerning my welfare. "You are not ready yet. You have to change what you eat first. You still eat too much meat and other things. You must be there to take care of Teluke and his family."

That was all I needed to know. I looked up at Teluke and smiled. "...I'm not afraid to die. But the last time I said that, I didn't have anything to live for. Things are different now. I need to be here for you guys." He smiled warmly at me, acknowledging my decision.

He occasionally spoke to me on his own when I was outdoors. It was becoming common that when I called for him or wanted him to come up to the barn, I would meet him inside the force field and walk with him up to the barn. He was still indignant much of the time, however he was softening.

He told me that he had tried what I had told him to try on the collie. I asked how it went and he said that it worked. He also said that he was ready to kill it if he had to, though. I told him I was glad for both of us that he did not have to. I didn't want him to be hurt and I also loved the dog and would miss him. But I told him that I would have understood if he had had to. He was proud when he reported that he had even petted him, but that he began to growl, so he quit.

One day as I spoke to Teluke up in the woods, my girlfriend, Nan, walked out to me into the field to ask which bridle to use on one of our horses. She had become used to seeing me standing out in the hayfield, so I always had numerous excuses handy these days. We conversed a few minutes laughing and she returned to the barn.

Teluke asked me, "What were you doing with your mouths?"

Talking, why?" I asked.

"That's not talking! There is only one way to talk," he said, meaning telepathically.

"No, there are many ways to talk. Some people are born who cannot talk with their mouths and so they use their hands to talk," I said patiently.

"What words were you using?"

"My friend and I were using the same words with our mouths that you and I are speaking now! Come out here and I will show you."

He climbed the fence and came out to me. I spoke to him, verbally. He was extremely intrigued and curious. "It sounds funny to hear it that way," he said.

"Would you like to try it? I will teach you," I offered.

Feeling rather pompous suddenly, he said, "I can do anything you can do! Yes! Teach me this talking with the mouth!"

I thought a moment as to a good place to start. Of course! Baby words! Babies say the easiest words to pronounce. I was familiar with the difficulties babies have with some words at first, so I started out simple.

"Ok, say Ma-Ma."

"What does that mean?" he asked me telepathically.

"That is what our babies call mother," I explained.

"I am not a baby!" He was insulted.

"Of course you're not! But you are just beginning to speak and it is hard to say mother, when you are just beginning. You can say mother if you want to, but it is harder," I explained.

So we went with "mother". I told him to watch my mouth and tongue as I said the word slowly.

"Now you try," I urged him. His voice was deep but my eyes were not seeing anything in front of me. I was going on pure faith that I wasn't nuts believing all of this. Hearing this deep voice in front of me, saying for its first time, 'mother', tickled me to the bone and I couldn't help but giggle! It was just so absurd hearing him, but not seeing him. The shock to my body, hearing, yet not seeing him, just startled me! His voice was pleasant enough and he said the word okay. It was the kind of thing Nan and I did all the time, laughing at ourselves in sort of an embarrassment when you feel funny.

He was appalled by me! With wide eyes he telepathed, "You laughed!"

"That was pretty good really! Try it again," I encouraged him honestly. But he was humiliated by my laughing and said he felt stupid. I told him he wasn't stupid at all. I told him that stupid is when a person won't try or cannot learn, which he was quite able to do. He was too embarrassed though, and though I felt bad, I understood. He said he wanted to bring his wife up to the barn to listen to this talking with the mouth sometime. I told him that was fine.

He had determined he was going to learn this "talking with the mouth" and seemed bent on proving to someone that he could do anything I could do. So, it shouldn't have come as a surprise later, when things were lighter between us that he spoke telepathically to me about it.

"We have a lot of fun trying to talk with our mouths back at our place," he revealed to me.

"What words are you saying?" I was genuinely curious. I had noticed several times that he had brought Teleel up to the barn doors when the barn was busy.

"Shit, ...god damn it, son of bitch ...", he rolled out a number of spicy words he had heard around the barn.

I started laughing in embarrassment. "Oh, man! Some teacher I am! You have picked out all the bad words people say around here! Don't learn those! Try saying 'I love you' to each other! Or, 'may I help you?' or something. Don't start out with those words," I smiled at him.

He asked what they mean and I explained them. I said he should not say words he did not understand.

I tried to encourage him to feel free to use his voice around me as well, but he seemed to think it was demeaning to make mistakes in my presence. I explained that my people do not think it is kind to make fun of people who have a hard time. I told him that there are people who never learn to say words right, and we do not make fun of them. But it was important to Teluke that he maintain his dignity, so I left him with his own choice about it and never mentioned it again.

# CHAPTER NINE

## Lowering the Shields

"I am the offspring of my thoughts

like a shadow in the sun

following my dreams aloft

the web of time has spun."

ARLY INTO OUR EXPOSURE TO one another, he had asked me if I knew which plants were good to eat around here. I really didn't know too much about it. I only knew of dandelions, "nuts and berries". But I told him I could get a book at the library and we could learn them together. He said he didn't need our books, that he would learn them by himself. He said that they were not from around here. They were from far away and the plants were different here.

One mid-morning I was sitting out at the barn facing the woods with a two-fold purpose. I wanted to attract his attention with my thoughts, but completely be minding my own business. It worked.

"Female!" His voice took command of me. "Where are you?"

"I'm out in the barn." I stood up and waved to the woods from the doorway.

"What is it that you are doing?" he asked.

"I am reading a book. Why?" I was tickled at my success.

"I have been listening to you." I found this humorous. He was too curious about me to reject me totally.

I asked, "Can you see the pictures as I look at them?"

He affirmed this, so I offered to read it and explain the pictures to him as I went. I was pleased. I felt as though he had sidled up next to me there on the stoop, though he had not.

We got to talking about geography and I asked him where he was from. He said it was very far away from here and assured me I had never heard of it and didn't want to bother telling me. I persisted and he said he wasn't sure he could say it right but it was Kun-Ta-Kee.

It sounded familiar and I played with it a moment before I realized the word and asked, "Kentucky?"

He lit up and came to life. He was amazed I had heard of it.

I responded, "Oh, yeah! It's not very far from here. I've been there before."

"It is far!" He seemed annoyed with me, so I explained.

"Well, I guess it is far if you are walking, but the way we travel I could be there in a few hours."

He asked what hours were. I explained to him the ticking of seconds and minutes and hours and a day's worth of hours. I told him that if I left right now in my car, I would be in Kentucky before the sun went down. I explained cars and other ways we travel and offered to give them a ride in the truck sometime, if they would like. I explained that we can travel all over the world and tried to explain the earth as a ball in the sky and asked if he knew of the great water that we call oceans and seas. He had heard of them. I told him that one day I had hoped to go see the oceans. That maybe I would fly in one of the airplanes, too! I told him that we put a man on the moon, but he didn't believe me. (I don't understand this when he travels by star ship, or even why Kentucky seemed far away to him.)

Teluke was in awe as I explained that we can go all the way around the world to any place on the globe. I knew it must be a bit overwhelming to him, so I offered to bring out a book that would show him the landmasses and the great waters.

I went in the house and retrieved an almanac and carried it out into the pasture. He had me lay it down near the fence and step back to the edge of the force field. As I did so, I placed a rock on the best page I wanted him to see, to hold it open for him. He wanted to know if he should keep the rock or what it was for. I told him it was just to hold the book open to the right page.

He paged through it right away and I tried to explain what he was probably looking at. I really had hoped he would invite me in so we could page through it together. I had no way of knowing what he was looking at unless he showed me telepathically, which he wasn't doing. His thoughts were to himself and his mate, so I couldn't share in this.

He found the book itself interesting, but what was inside didn't make too much sense to him. He asked what the other stuff in the book was, that was not pictures. And I explained they were written words I could read, or understand. He was amazed.

"They said you people have lots of magic," he exclaimed.

He asked if we had anymore books and I said yes, and went in the house to bring out more. I knew picture books were what was called for, but Mom and Pop didn't have a library at all. So I took some unimportant books along with a few magazines and a horse almanac out to them.

Once again I had hoped to be invited into their "place" and visit, but as usual he had me bring them to the fence and go away. He asked if they could keep them for a while, and I said yes. "I can let you have them overnight if you want! But try not to get them wet so they don't get ruined. Water will harm them." They thanked me and said they would take care of them for me.

The next day when I came for them, Teluke was really upset. The books had gotten damp from dew and waffled. He called it "rain that happens every night and makes the ground wet."

I looked at them and they weren't that bad at all. I offered to bring some more books out to them. He refused for fear they might get ruined also, but said his wife really liked the pretty horses and thanked me for letting them look at them. He sincerely apologized again. I was touched by his concern.

I wanted to speak to Teleel, but he was still very much protecting her from me. I had not attempted to contact her for fear he would carry out his threat to kill her. When I approached the force field to communicate with Teluke, I could hear her private thoughts, hoping I would not speak to her. In my own private thoughts I would then think to myself in return, "No, honey, I will not allow him to harm you because of me." These being my own private thoughts, they were available if one broke etiquette and 'looked' in, but they were not being sent out. So just as her wishes were known to me safely, she too had access to my intentions.

But for a good while now, he had so shielded her by some barrier that cut me off from her words to him and for that matter, her own private thoughts, that I could no longer pick her up telepathically. It was something like "out of sight, out of mind."

One afternoon I went into the pasture for a visit. It was starting to get pretty hot during the days. "May I come visit you?" I had tried to be polite so he would see my real intent.

"Yes," came his reply as I walked out into the field.

"Why are you always cooking?" he asked me.

My thoughts turned to the house. Was he watching me in the privacy of my home again? But that didn't make sense either.

"But I don't cook. Hardly ever! Mom does all the cooking. I've asked to help, but she always tell me no". I was perplexed by this.

"Then why are you always eating?"

"I'm not always eating."

"Yes you are! You are eating right now!"

What was he talking about? "No, I hardly eat at all! I only eat three times a day with the family and I don't eat much then! If I ate all the time I would get fat!"

Teluke was disgusted with me. "Oh, why do I even bother with you?" I felt him turn away.

"Please!" I begged him. "I don't understand! Don't get mad! I don't know what you are talking about. Please explain this to me!" I was afraid of losing ground on his trust again.

"Then what is in your hand?"

I looked and started to laugh. "Oh! I'm not eating this! I'm breathing it! I'm smoking a cigarette! This is a cigarette!" He was attentive again.

"Why do you do this? Is it hot? I see smoke coming out of your mouth," he asked curiously.

"No, it isn't hot until it gets short. I do it partly because I enjoy it, and partly because I have to. My body is addicted to it. It gets afraid if I stop for long." I went on to explain, "It's not good for me. I should quit and I plan to sometime."

"Why do you do it if it is not good for you?" he asked me.

"Well," I said, "when I was real little I saw people on television and they were having a wonderful time by the ocean, and a man's voice came on and said I would get more out of life if I smoked these. I believed him. And, because I wanted to get the most out of life, I chose right then that when I grew up I was going to smoke. But the truth is that I will get a shorter life and illness from it! They didn't tell me that."

He was disgusted by our people again. "Why would they tell a lie to their own children and let them do something that hurts them? Your people are bad!"

I explained that they didn't all know it was dangerous. But some of them made a lot of money on it and kept it to themselves. It was more important to them to be rich than to look into what they were doing to us. "All they saw was money."

"I've heard about money," he said.

"So now there are whole generations of people that are addicted and harming themselves with it," I went on. "It isn't that they lie to their own children. It would be like me lying to your children and you lying to mine."

"I would not lie to your children!" Teluke defended.

"And I wouldn't lie to your children either. But this is basically what they did to us."

"What is it you smoke in there?" he asked.

"It is a plant."

"Oh, how can that be a plant? That's not a plant." He questioned me. He was becoming distrustful again.

"Yes, it is made from a plant called tobacco. Do you know tobacco?"

"Yes, I know tobacco."

I saw tobacco barns from his old stomping grounds flash through my head. I broke a cigarette open into my palm and looked at it, showing him telepathically. I said, "A long time ago, when my skin was red, I and my people honored this plant. It is sacred to us and we respect it. So when I was born into this white body, I was naturally attracted to it. But, this race of people taught me how to abuse the sacred plant before I realized what I was doing. Now the plant has taken revenge and has control of my body. My body hurts and gets scared if I don't put my attention back on the plant by smoking it."

We were both enjoying the company. It was getting hot lying in the field and I said, "You sure are lucky you don't have to wear clothes! They are hot!"

"Why don't you take them off then?" he asked sincerely.

"I wish I could, but I am ashamed of my body. Plus, we have rules, you know."

Teluke was dumbfounded by this remark. "Ashamed of your body? That doesn't make sense! It is the one you were given to use! You should be happy to have it!"

"Yes, I know, and I try to be. But you tell me I look stupid with my clothes on and my people tell me I took stupid with them off, so how am I supposed to feel about myself?"

He was silent for a moment, then added, "Why do your people tell you you look stupid with them off? Don't you ever take them off? Do you sleep in them? Doesn't your mate see you with them off?"

"Yes, we take them off to clean our bodies with water and before we go to sleep at night, but no one else is supposed to see us without them. Just family, brother and sisters while we are young, then only our mates after we grow up. 'They' pick a certain person from TV and tell us their bodies are perfect and that we should try to look that way, too. Every once in a while they change people we're supposed to look like. A long time ago women were supposed to be plump."

"What is 'plump'?" Teluke asked.

"Plump is like you. Nice and round." I went on, "Then later they changed it to be small at the middle and have big breasts. Now the breasts aren't so important, but you gotta' be skinny." I was getting depressed.

"This is stupid! How can you change your body?"

"That's just it! You can't very much! You can lose some weight or gain some weight, but some people are born with big bones and some with little bones. They can only do so much. Some people will never have large breasts and some will always have them. Only small differences are usually made. If you happen to be given a body that is fairly close to what they are calling perfect at the time, you can make the adjustment. The rest are miserable with themselves."

He was disgusted, as I too was. "I would not like having someone tell me everything I can do."

I relaxed in the sun and unbuttoned my shirt a little to catch a breeze. "It feels so good to talk this way, instead of how my people talk with the mouth!"

"You do it well," he commented.

"I talk to my people this way, but they don't usually hear me. Do you know why?"

Teluke couldn't figure it out either.

I told him we have complicated life terribly. He wanted to know what "complicated" was.

"Complicated means hard to put together. Like if I broke a rock into three pieces, it would be easy to put back together."

"Oh, how could you put a rock back together?" he broke in.

"Ha, believe me, we can do it! But, if I broke the rock and shattered it into many tiny pieces, it would be very complicated, maybe impossible, to put back together right. See?" I went on, "You have kept life simple for yourselves. There are many of my people who do not wish to live this way anymore. We get mad about being lied to and having rules that are stupid. Some of us want to eat food that is not poisoned with sugar and chemicals. But there seems to be more foolish people here than good ones, and the foolish ones seem to make the rules.

For some reason, <u>most</u> of the people want sugar and poison. So the food that is clean and good for you is real expensive to make up for not selling so much of it. You can't afford to eat the good food! And we don't know any other way to live!"

"We would like very much for someone to help us return to a life like yours. We would be willing to live a harder life that was good for us instead of a soft life that makes us sick. We control the air in our homes so that it is cool inside when it is hot outside, and we keep it warm inside the house, when it is cold outside. It makes it hard on our bodies then, to go outdoors at all! Some of my people are learning to know plants and learning to return to the old ways of doing things, but it is very slow and hard to do alone. I would like this myself, but I just don't even know how to start it."

Teluke and I often frequented each other's company. It was a pleasure to see him heading up to the barn when he saw me heading out there. In the evening when it started getting dark, I stood at the rail talking to him before going on in the house.

"Why are you hitting yourself?" he asked.

"The bugs are eating me alive! Aren't they bothering you?"

He seemed to never have heard such an odd thing and said no. He wanted me to stay out and play, but the bugs chased me in. I told him that as much as I hated it, I could buy a can of bug spray to put on, so the bugs would leave me alone. Then I could stay out after dark longer. He told me that they just get started when it gets dark and was sorry I always went in then. I asked when they go to sleep and he said just before the birds sing.

I knew about what time they get up because one morning I had gone out there bright and early, about 7:00 or 8:00 a.m., and asked if he was up. After a moment, his quiet voice said he was asleep and he would let me know when he awoke, which had been about 10:00 a.m.

This one quiet country afternoon, I was sitting in the yard swing, listening to the musical buzzing of insects. I was enjoying the pleasant balmy air, when Teluke ask me if he could have some of the chickens to eat.

"Man, I wished you hadn't asked me that, Teluke! You should have just taken one. I would give you anything I have, but those are Pop's chickens, not mine to give you."

I thought a moment, I really wanted him to eat decently. "Tell you what. I'm gonna' forget you asked me, and I will close my eyes while you do what you need to do. I don't want to know anything about it. Okay?"

"Oh, how can you not know?" he asked, disbelieving. He seemed puzzled by it as I closed my eyes and sat in the swing.

The chicken ladies cackled and screamed and it became unnerving to me and impossible to ignore and to "not know" anything about it, so I got up and went in the house so "I wouldn't know".

When Pop went out to feed that night, he said someone had gotten one of his chickens. I suggested it must be a fox or something, but he was sure about it. "No, this was a man. He cleaned it right there in the pen."

He was concerned about it, but I don't believe he ever connected it with whoever had looked into the windows periodically. Each seemed to be a mystery of its own. And there was no shortage of mysteries these days.

I felt badly, but didn't know what to do from here except make myself scarce. Teluke had a right to feed his family, and they would not survive in that tiny woods without some help.

The next time Teluke came for a chicken, I told him not to clean it there. "Take it out in the woods or somewhere to do it. The chicken ladies shouldn't see that, anyway! They have to live with that vision and knowing they saw their sister die a horribly frightening death. It will make them live in fear that they may be next. Take it into the woods or into the other world so no one will see the feathers and stuff. That way no one will be able to trace it back to you. Pop found the remains of the last one and he was upset about it. He may not have even noticed if he hadn't seen that."

Teluke went over to the pen and leaped the tall fence from a standstill like a gazelle. The chickens went wild as I watched the invisible man corralling the hens. He caught one and flipped her over into the other dimension. It appeared to have knocked her out as she hung lifeless by her feet in his hand.

Teluke strolled out through the pasture. The hen had come back to consciousness and was screaming helplessly into another world, flapping her little wings above her head as she dangled head down. I felt so bad for her. "Bless her heart." I sent my thoughts to her and picked up Teluke's thoughts to himself as he heard mine, "Well, we have to eat."

"He's gotten another one of my chickens," Pop told me with concern. He wasn't mad about it, yet, just concerned. I knew that if it kept up, he would be.

"He got my best layer too!" he said.

I had to tell Teluke that he had better not take any more chickens so we could avoid trouble. He was somewhat disgusted because we had so much to eat and they had so little. I agreed that it wasn't right. If they had been mine, I would have shared them, but Pop had taken his own time to raise, feed and care for them, and spent his hard-earned money to do it and so he deserved the right to claim them for himself. I told Teluke that if he raised and took care of some he could have his own too, but he said no.

He asked what those other birds are that we have in the other 'place'. I told him they were Peacocks. He liked them and found them especially pretty. He liked birds and had never seen those before. He asked why we have them locked up so they aren't free. I explained it was for their own safety so fox and dogs or a car won't kill them. He seemed to understand.

# CHAPTER TEN

## Two Steps Forward, One Step Back

*"Sometimes its just a matter*

*of how you translate the sunshine."*

O N SOME LEVELS, TELUKE WAS beginning to understand that I meant well and I tried hard not to give him any reason to doubt my intentions, though mistakes were sometimes made. Things were beginning to relax a bit between us.

One evening I talked with him about the Creator and reincarnation. He seemed to understand these topics well and seemed to have plenty of information about it, taking them as a natural "given". He was surprised that I knew much of what he knew and said I was "smarter than most people". How he derived this I don't know, save word of mouth about our society. I didn't believe this, but I knew I differed from others in that I spoke from the heart. I told him once when we were deep into the subject of reincarnation, that I used to be one of his people. This made him upset. He insisted my people could not be born into their bodies. I told him that I was sure I had been, but this was a very long time ago. He insisted it could never have been.

I assured him that at one time I was one with them. We went around and around about it as I drew on old knowledge. Finally I said that maybe I was speaking of the very beginning, when we were all a part of the same ball of wax, when we were one with the Creator. This was too far removed from either of us to argue anymore, so we dropped it peacefully.

Some of his ideas of knowledge on Spiritual things sounded like good ideas to me. I found a lot of truth in his knowledge. But, I was a bit leery to just accept them completely at that time. I told him that maybe one day I could let go of my fear, in my beliefs, as I would like to believe in these new things. But right now I still had much to learn yet. Maybe I would grow into them. The biggest difference was our belief in the Devil, which he said was not an entity.

I lit a cigarette and we began discussing fire. He wondered about my lighter and asked to see it. He bent the fence down, stepped over the fence, and walked up to me. I always played with my double perception at times like these, to see how it might look to others, for instance, seeing his steps flatten plants down when there was no breeze to blame it on.

I handed him my lighter and showed him how it worked. I explained to him how to hold his thumb out of the way so it wouldn't get burned. He found it interesting, but asked why we just don't make fire the right way, like they do.

I asked how that was and he gave me the impression of energy and combustion. I told him that we are not able to do that anymore and asked him if he would show me how they do this sometime. He agreed to.

That evening he spoke quietly to me in my head, while I was in the house with the family, and asked me if I wanted to watch him make fire. Not knowing what might be involved, I excused myself from the family and said yes.

I sat on the edge of the bathtub and telepathically watched from his eyes as he sat in camp. I would like to explain that their eyesight is such that it bleeds out the darkness such as our present night-scopes can do. Their eyes remove darkness so that even on the blackest of nights, they see things quite clearly.

I saw the log he focused on quite easily because of this. It began to hiss and smoke and insects ran out of the bark in a hurry. I heard Teluke tell them, "Yes, you better get out of there!" I could see energy filling the log in one spot and felt an urgency in the wood. It popped and squeaked and turned red just before a beautiful flame sprung out, lighting the area for them.

"Did you see that?" he asked me.

"Yes! That was neat! Thank you! We cannot do that! You are lucky!" I asked him if he could show me how to do that and he said he didn't know if he could or not.

I asked him how he would teach a child and he said he would just say, "Do this". That left me feeling rather hopeless to learn how. I did step outside then, and show him what the dark time looked like to us. It happened to be especially dark that night and I was more blind than usual, having just come from inside. He was rather surprised at how blind we are at night. Once more he showed me how clearly he could see out on the pasture in the night-light.

I began to notice a change in the Collie dog over the weeks. He gradually stopped growling and/or barking. Eventually he would trot into the pasture and stop, and then wag his tail. Sometimes the dog wouldn't notice Teluke until Teluke was in the paddock beside the garden fence. I would hear Teluke calmly say no to the dog and the dog would stop where he was and just wag his tail at Teluke. I sensed a swelling of pride in Teluke at learning how to handle the dog.

I had stopped opening the garden-pasture gate because Teluke had taken it upon himself to just swing underneath the two corner paddock rails to enter the garden.

"Your people have good food," he told me one day when I was riding along the rail.

I smiled at him as he hunkered down near the corner to eat and watch me ride. My palomino mare was always nervous around him, but if the Sasquatch stayed put and given a wide berth, I could get her to ignore them pretty much.

"Which food do you like best?" I asked him.

"My wife likes this long food," he said as he ate a carrot. "That round food is bad. We don't like it!"

I laughed, "You mean onions? Yeah, a lot of people can't handle them. But they are good when they are cooked. Then they aren't hot inside anymore, but turn real sweet!"

"Do you ever eat insects?" I was curious about their normal diet.

"Oh, nobody eats those!" he said, after I explained what they were.

To them insects were just something you brush off your food. He had no name for them.

I told him that there are some people who do roast bugs to eat. I said they are supposed to be very good for you to eat, but I probably would rather starve than eat them.

He had squatted by the rail and was eating a carrot happily, like a child with a peanut butter sandwich, watching contentedly as I worked my mare. I pulled up near him and let my mare play out a comfortable distance from him until she would stand quietly.

I was awestruck. He was just so beautiful to me - so animal looking, yet so very human at the same time. His white teeth glistened as he chewed. His expression was of simplicity and casual contentment. It struck me humorous that he could talk with a full mouth since he was telepathing.

"My God, you are beautiful to me! You're so 'gorilla," I said honestly. He seemed about to be offended. "Don't get mad! I know you are human, but your body is so gorilla-like! I think it's wonderful! I think gorillas and all life forms are beautiful. I like the way you look! You are beautiful to me!"

I told him that I would find a picture of a gorilla to show him sometime. "I love you!" I smiled and nudged my horse to move on. I was so honored to have this opportunity! Even if he was human, it was as close as I would probably ever come to being near a gorilla. He was awesome, breathtaking in every way. Looking into his human eyes when caught off guard or was allowed to, it was so unreal to see a man beneath there. "I think you are the most beautiful creation God ever made!" I told him.

When later I did bring out a picture of a gorilla, he took a double take. "I thought it was a man I know!" he said.

I giggled. "Seeee! You look like a gorilla!"

"There's an animal that looks just like me! May I take this back to show my wife?" he asked. Naturally, I said yes. He never got upset about the comparison again.

At the onset of our acquaintance he had asked me about the animals up at the barn, and I told them they were horses. He wanted to know what we do with them and I told him we ride them to exercise them. I told him that they enjoy it as much as we do and said that we love horses. We just enjoy them to work with and be around.

He had thought we were being mean to them when we didn't have time to ride and instead, worked the herd as a group with a whip, forcing them to work off some energy and steam. I explained that they like the excitement and get bored with nothing to do and that sometimes they just look for something to blow up over. "They are people, too. They have feelings and get depressed or lonely or bored. Having good humans makes their life richer and rewarding and they appreciate being worked and handled every day. It is a mutual giving to each other."

He said they were pretty and he liked them. He wanted to know if he might be able to ride one sometime.

"Sure! I would be happy to teach you! I give riding lessons." I explained that the horses would probably be afraid of him, so he should focus on just one mare.

"What is mare?" he questioned.

"That is a female horse."

"What do you call a male horse?" he wondered. He always liked to know our words.

"We call the male a stallion!" I was pleased to just say the beautiful word.

"Stallion! That is a good name! I like stallion!" He tested the word out a couple of times. I wasn't about to tell him about geldings.

I said to pick a mare that didn't seem as afraid of him as the others were. I told him to let her get used to seeing him, smelling him, and if he could, to try to feed her a handful of grass or grain. I told him the big brown mare would likely be his best choice.

"She is the one in the barn next to the yellow mare. The yellow mare is mine and she is a screwball. You probably won't get close to her, she is afraid of her drinking water!" I laughed at the thought of the silly mare trembling if I approached her with a bucket of water or a hose, or even a teaspoon of medicine.

Teluke couldn't understand how she could be afraid of her water, but he was pleased to have my consent.

Later he asked me if that was my mate he saw in the barn. I told him yes.

"He is not very big. He is ....long," he commented, haltingly.

"Yeah!" I smiled lovingly. "You mean he is tall! I like him that way," I said, swooning over my honey.

Teluke didn't' seem to see what I saw so attractive in Byron, but went on with his point.

"He is good to his horse. I like listening to him talk to it. He is not like you. You are not good to yours."

I understood why he thought that. I smiled at him. "I am good to her. I love my mare very much! I fell in love with horses the very first time I saw one and it was the very first thing I bought when I was out on my own. You must understand that she is very big and I am very little. She tries to push me around and I must stand my ground so she doesn't know she is bigger than me. Right now she doesn't know that! If she found it out, I would not be able to control her and she would be dangerous to me. If you notice, I am not that way with the other horses."

"But your mate is not mean to her," he came back.

"He keeps her in line when she needs it. He is bigger, so she doesn't try to get away with as much with him. I am only this way with her. She is the one I love most because she belongs to me."

I was truly pleased with the progress we had made. I went out one day and was standing with Teluke in the hay. We were having a pleasant conversation and I asked how my baby was, speaking metaphorically.

"Your baby? You have a baby?" He seemed shocked.

"Yeah! Your baby is my baby! I'm just letting you raise her for me!" I teased.

It was the wrong thing to do! He took me dead serious and told me I was going to try to steal her and he would never trust me around them. He had been bringing them up to the barn occasionally with him, but that all dried up right then. He said he would kill me if I ever got near them!

I knew he meant it. I tried to explain that babies belong to everybody! That they are a blessing to be shared! That she was only mine because I was connected to her by love. I said that I loved her as if she was my own and that the women in our family shared our babies because they are to be loved and held and kissed. I told him that I would never take their baby away because I do love her and knew her mother was the best one to care for her.

He told me that sometimes my people try to steal their children and he would never trust me around them again.

And so it broke my heart when the family came up one day to observe us and I was so glad to see Teleel and the baby that I had forgotten the discussion. I guess I couldn't believe I had not gotten through to him my honesty and sincerity. I rushed over anxiously to greet them and was charged.

Teleel cowered behind Teluke in fear for her child and Teluke's attitude was not to be questioned. What really hurt though, was that Teleel was now terrified of me. I was distraught.

The only way to prove myself was to toe the line. I had to be impeccable in my action to prove to them I would never hurt them that way. My intentions were pure. My brain was forgetful. I had to make my body disobey what my heart felt and my heart was always so full of love and anticipation, that I would mistakenly look at them or move at them for an instant.

Every time he did bring them up from then on, I was ordered to stay away from her, and she would cower if I looked in her direction. This hurt me to the quick. I loved that baby so much I could hardly stand it, especially since Bryon wouldn't let us create one of our own.

My arms burned to just hold her or touch her tiny fingers and kiss her fuzzy brow. And now I wasn't even allowed to look at them! It was very painful. I wanted one of my own so badly that it was a release to hold someone else's.

I was extremely envious of Byron's brother's new child and held it a great deal when they came over. But I set myself to work on keeping my eyes from them as best I could. I wanted them to know my integrity.

Other than that, things were decent between Teluke and I when the family was not around. When they were, he was on guard all the time and I was working diligently to be impeccable, even when I failed.

One day I was riding in the pasture when I caught sight of Teluke running on all fours. He was bounding playfully up towards the woods. Seeing him this way played confusion with my head as to what it was. I could have sworn his feet were not long and human, but had become round paws instead. He telepathed to me that it was him. And he was always especially ornery in this state. He felt good.

One evening, when Byron was with me, Teluke must have felt exuberant and came bounding up on all fours and before I knew what had happened, he struck me in the forehead with his paws, knocking me down. Byron ran to my aid and helped me up as I rubbed my forehead. Teluke's scratchy paws were the painful part. I could feel telepathically that it wasn't done maliciously. It was out of pure abandonment, the way a child would go on swinging in a swing if it unintentionally knocked another child down.

It was not at all unlike an incident when my male Great Dane came running down the path behind me. We both stepped aside simultaneously and he plowed me down, galloped across my back and disappeared on up the way, never looking back to see why the road had been so bumpy back there.

But to see them on all fours was probably as unnerving to me as anything they did. They looked inhuman at those times, reminding me of bears. This was true Shape Shifting.

One evening I saw them both playing this way in the hayfield. They were tumbling and wrestling, charging each other and running from each other. I asked if they were fighting, but they said no, they were having fun and continued. I sat on my mare observing and could see it was much the way dogs play and chase and roll each other.

The baby was clinging to her mother's chest as Teleel held her with one arm. They would leap and run and attack and roll...and giggle.

I asked if it didn't hurt their backs to do that for so long a time, but Teleel said no. Teluke called her back into the game. I could hear her talk to the baby during the mock fight, saying "Here he comes! Let's get out of the way," and then leap and roll away from the attack and Teluke would let them get away.

It looked like so much fun! I had often wished I could run on all fours along side my dogs. Four legs gave one such freedom of expression!

"Can I play, too?" I asked in anticipation.

"You have your horse," Teluke said coldly.

"Oh, I can turn her loose and she will go on up to the barn."

"No," he said flatly. "You go play with your own people. You are not one of us. You have plenty of people to play with. We only have each other." Teleel got up and headed towards the woods. I had broken the mood and she was through. Teluke was disgusted that I had disturbed their game.

His words stung me and I felt bad that I had caused it to end. But, since it was over, I was still curious. "How do you put your leg? Show me where you put it? I would like to learn how to do that," I asked.

Teluke bent back down into position. It almost seemed to make his thigh, from the knee to the hip, disappear.

"Where do you put your leg? I couldn't tell if they carried it underneath the body or beside it, because of the hair.

"You know!" he said. "You put your leg in that place."

"You mean there is a place you put it, like it holds it there or locks in place or something?" I asked. I could see then it was alongside the body and that they just use from the knee down.

He looked at me curiously and said yes.

"We can't do that. Our leg doesn't go into any "place" like that. Our bodies must be made differently," I said sadly, and headed on up to the barn.

He had mentioned one day that he was a medicine man, a doctor, and I asked what all he could do. He said he could do everything.

"Can you heal broken bones?" I asked.

"Well, yes, sometimes," he halted.

"If a person loses an arm can you put it back on?"

"No," he said in a curious way. He was wondering where I was going with it.

"Our doctors can, if the arm isn't ruined. They can't if it's messed up badly," I explained. "But we make arms for those people then, out of plastic."

"Can you take a heart out and put in a new one?" I asked.

"Oh, no one can do **that**!" he said defensively.

"Our doctors can. I'm pretty sure of it," I told him.

"I don't believe you!" His skepticism was hard to overcome.

"I'm pretty sure they can! Come up to the barn tonight. My girlfriend is coming over later, and I will ask her in front of you and you will hear it from someone else. I will pretend I don't know."

When Nan came over that night, I called Teluke up to the barn. He stood cautiously by the door.

"Nan, am I correct that doctors can take someone's heart out and put in a new one from somebody else who is almost ready to die?" I asked, scratching my head and ignoring Teluke.

She chuckled at the seriousness of my question. "Yeah, I think so! They do heart by-passes and stuff. I think they can do heart transplants," and she went on into some of the details.

"They can't do that with the brain yet, can they?" I asked, so the conversation wouldn't look suspicious.

We both broke out laughing, "No, I don't think they can do that yet!"

"I gave Teluke a "See! I told you so!" expression, and ignored him, freeing him to return to the woods. He left with a puzzled idea of our "magic", as he called it.

The next day we had the blacksmith out to trim the horses' feet. Teluke wanted to know all the details about this, which I explained. He asked about the blacksmith's hat, which was a ball cap.

"I like your hats better. It makes you look like somebody," he said.

"Who is that?" I asked, thinking he had somebody in mind.

"Not somebody like that. It looks important. I think I would like to have one someday."

I chuckled, but felt the need to warn him, "Now don't get carried away on appearances. It is real easy to think that what a person has on their body makes them how they really are. People are aware of this illusion and sometimes dress to fool others. Any body can get the proper clothes to fill a role they may not be real in. You must remember who you are, and that you are already important!" I cautioned him.

# CHAPTER ELEVEN

## An Effort To Succeed

*"…In frothy phosphorescent waves*

*as milkweed babies fly*

*to encompass a seeking heart*

*and leave behind a sigh…"*

EVENTUALLY TELUKE ASKED ME IF I would take him and his family for a ride in the truck. Knowing they were each almost the size of a refrigerator and not knowing how much they weighed, I decided to put them in the truck bed rather than the cab.

He brought Teleel and the baby up to the barn. Naturally they were all invisible to the eye, but I never had trouble seeing them anyway. He asked how far I would take them. I told him just down the road and back.

"How do I know you will bring us back?" he asked warily.

I laughed at his simplicity. "Well if I don't, you can hurt me with your mind to stop me. You are not as helpless as you feel."

His constant state of feeling vulnerable proved his good heart. He was scared of me even though by all rights, he had no reason to be. They always felt defenseless unless provoked. This is where their purity lies. Their natural state of innocence always kept them one step removed from their actual power.

I had no reason to fear telling him this because I knew myself. I had no intention of betraying their trust in me. I know that state of vulnerability and had compassion for them.

He seemed to think it was safe when I reminded him of his defense. I didn't have to worry, I knew he would do me no unjust harm.

I opened the bed of the truck and turned and glanced at them as a natural beginning. She cowered into Teluke and he said in exasperation, "Don't look at us!"

I apologized for forgetting my manners, and they climbed in, weighing the truck down significantly!

They sat at the rear as I explained to them, "Now you need to know the safety rules. Please stay sitting down while the truck is moving or you will fall out and get hurt badly! People die all the time from these accidents. If you get scared do not jump out! Tell me if you get scared and I will stop, or slow down or come back home, but don't try to get out while we are moving! The pavement is very hard and will break bones if you land on it from a fall. OK? Just don't jump out! I don't want you to get hurt!"

I told them that the truck bed door was noisy so to expect it while I shut it, and not to be afraid. Everything was fine. Teleel was preparing the baby for an adventure, talking to it softly, and we pulled out.

What a riot! I was having a ball! I got out on the road and saw in the mirror, into the other dimension, that their hair was flying furiously and since that was seen psychically, I giggled at the absurdity of this whole thing!

When I got up to about 40 mph, Teluke said they could not breathe. I told them to cup their hands over their mouths and noses. I told them it was normal and it happens to everyone. I explained that it was because of the air coming at them so fast.

They were getting a little afraid, even though we had only gone possibly a half-mile. But they wanted to turn around and go home. I slowed down and was watching for a place to turn around when Teluke sent pain into my head. It was excruciating! Everything else blanked out of my mind and I grabbed my head with my hands.

"**What** are you **doing**?" I yelled.

"I said go back home!" Teluke ordered

"I am! I have to go a little further to find a place to turn around! Look at the size of the road and the truck! There is no room to turn here!" I was mad! I didn't deserve this! But I did understand that he didn't know why we were continuing on. I had stepped on the brake to avoid any accident in my pain, when he stopped it. I turned around and returned home. He apologized to me and I let it go. I understood his position.

When we got back, I put the tailgate down and they thanked me and got out, much to the joy and relief of my poor truck! We began discussing the trip. He said it smelled bad.

I told him it does, and that it is poisonous if you breathe it directly. Fear crossed Teluke's face, that I had purposely harmed them, but I assured him that he was safe because he had plenty of fresh air mixed with it.

I went on to explain that it is why the air is getting dirty now because we have too much of it. He wanted to know why we don't stop using it then and I said because we don't have a better way to travel but are looking for a cleaner way. He seemed to understand.

He liked the ride and said that if I could drive a truck, then he knew he could, too! He said he could do anything I could do! He wanted to know if I would let him drive it.

I thought about the complications of a beginner with a stick shift and told him that I didn't think he should drive the truck to start off with. I said it would be better to drive Pop's automatic. He became pompous and said he wanted to drive the truck, because I had.

I glanced at Teleel's feet with a question. "What's he trying to prove?"

Her answer was that she was just as curious about it. She didn't know why men always have to prove something either.

"Look!" I said taking control of the situation. "I know you can drive! You don't have to prove anything to me! But I want you to succeed!"

"What is succeed?" he asked me.

"I want you to be able to do it well! You would be better off to drive Pop's car because most of it is done for you! With the truck, you have to keep each hand and foot doing something different all at one time. With Pop's car all you have to think about is driving! That is enough for someone to start with! I won't let you drive the truck first! You want to be able to do it well, don't you?"

"Yes." He seemed to see I meant what I said and accepted it.

When he saw Pop come home from work, he reminded me to ask him for the car. They came up to the barn and I went in to get the keys. When I returned, I suggested that Teleel and the baby not go because they would be safer left behind. I was willing to die, but they need not.

"No. She goes too. If I die, we all go together," he said sternly. This made me angry because he didn't even consider how she felt about it.

I turned towards her, keeping my eyes on the ground, for her opinion.

"I don't want to be here alone," she said softly. "I would be afraid."

I told them it was their choice and so I backed the car onto the road and parked it. I put Teleel and the baby in the back seat because it was safer. Once they were in, I told Teluke that I needed to put the seat belt on her.

He okayed this but warned me not to try anything as he stood close, ready to strike me if needed.

I had her put the baby beside her on the seat and scoot herself between the belt ends. I unrolled it almost all the way, to make it fit.

It was precious being so close to her, my hair brushed into hers as I leaned over her. She smelled so clean and sweet. If you have ever stuck your nose on a cow and was surprised how sweet they actually smell, or buried your nose into a clean house pet, this gives you some idea of her scent. Only the male Sasquatch smells bad.

Her vibrations were so radiant and different from Teluke's. As I buckled her in I told her privately, "God, you are precious honey!" Her naked body sat there so innocently. I couldn't help observe her breasts and lap while I buckled her in. She was so real. I showed her how to unbuckle it and had her try it so she could free herself if she needed to. The buckle fell open and I snapped it shut once more and glanced at the delightful baby sitting happily on the seat beside her before shutting the door for them.

I put Teluke behind the wheel. The car was significantly weighted down with the three of them in it. I realized this might be hard on pop's car and told him not to touch anything until I explained things.

"First off, don't go fast or you will get us all killed! Second, when I tell you to stop, just do it, then you can ask questions about it! We are breaking a big rule by letting you drive without a license. That is a piece of paper that says you have been tested to see if you know what you are doing and that you know the rules. If we get caught doing this by the wrong person, I will go to jail and really get in bad trouble."

He asked what jail was, so as I told him I telepathed a picture of me in a striped suit, with my hands on the bars as I peered out of a cell. He said sorrowfully, that he didn't want them to do that to me! Teleel agreed with him.

"You have to promise me that you will do everything I tell you to and not argue! If we have a wreck, I have to take all the blame myself!"

He seemed to understand and agreed, so I explained how to work the gas and brake and to put it in drive. I told him that the road belongs to everybody and that he had to share it by staying on one side. We rolled off and I had him try the brake to get the feel of them.

Without hesitation he put full thrust of his huge foot on the minuscule brake pedal and we all slammed forward. I cracked my head on the windshield and was momentarily knocked "conscious", if you will.

For an instant I realized and questioned that I was on the passenger side of the front seat in a moving vehicle with no driver! Then my mind changed frequencies and pickup up the Second Attention where it all made sense again and I saw the whole story.

I realized his strength was overpowering and explained that the car is made for us weaker humans and to be very gentle with the pedals. I told him to touch them very softly with his toes. He tried it again and was much better with it. I worried that he could put his foot right through Pop's floorboard easily!

We pulled out slowly and weaved back and forth across the road. It began to dawn on me how serious this was. I was sitting in a moving car, on the wrong side of the seat and my body was seeing no driver. The stress to my physical body was increasing each minute. I was trusting myself to something that at that moment, since I was really operating in a conscious manner, I wasn't real secure about. If someone saw me doing this, I couldn't explain it. I just prayed we wouldn't see a cop!

Very shortly a truck came barreling down the road towards us. We spent as much time on one side of the road as the other, so I began screaming at Teluke to get over to our side of the road. He began to argue with me, and I ordered him to the edge and to stop the car before he got us all killed! That seemed to sink in and he obeyed me. The truck whizzed by and we collected ourselves and went on.

I didn't know you could have a white-knuckle ride going 15 mph, but I sure was. I took a deep breath and tried to relax. He began doing better and we tootled along at 25, then 30 mph. Then came a car behind us. I told him to slow down and let her go around us and that I needed him to ignore me for I had to make it look like someone was driving the car.

I scooted over to him and put my arm across his back while I put my other hand on the wheel. Two old ladies were inside the passing car smiling and waving.

The driver was ignorant of her second sight but was acting on impulse because of her friend's excitement. You could see she was perplexed, by her expression, and that she saw nothing, but her passenger friend seemed pleasantly surprised to find this unusual being behind the wheel of my car and waved furiously at us as she said things to her friend.

We smiled and waved back. Teluke said, "Those were nice females," but I was heavily stressed and told him to keep his mind off women and on his driving.

When we reached the corner, I told him to stop. He put his foot on the peddle so carefully that it was taking too long and I realized I hadn't explained where at a corner he was expected to stop, or why. Our county line road intersected another county road that was traveled often by speeding cars, so I was approaching coronary by the time we came to a stop half way around the turn. I was sweating and trembling that we would meet another car.

A nervous wreck, I insisted I drive us back home. He really wanted badly to drive us back home saying he thought he had done pretty well, but I reminded him he had agreed to do what I told him to, and said I couldn't handle any more. He seemed pacified at having driven at all, so we exchanged places and went home, safely.

A few days later we took a trip to Evansville, IN and my sister-in-law complained that someone very big had used her seat belt in back. I just sat there feigning ignorance of it all. I took a deep breath, swallowed my tongue and peered out the window of the front seat.

# Chapter Twelve

## Hungry To Learn

"...*sometimes he hides in moonlight*

*sits at the base of trees*

*along the path where I will pass*

*to have me lock my knees...*"

AFTER THAT, THINGS AT THE farm seemed to be rolling along smoothly. Teluke wasn't getting me into trouble and I wasn't having to annoy him all the time because he was coming up to me more frequently.

He was pleased with his attempts to learn some of our ways, and looked for more challenges. Apparently having lost the battle to me damaged his self esteem a little, thus he needed to prove himself.

He asked me how that "other female goes along?" I telepathically saw from him my sister-in-law riding her bike on the road. So I explained it to him. He asked me, "Do you think I could try that?"

"Well, actually, no. Bikes aren't made to hold your weight. You would probably bend the wheels. The tires are filled with air and they squish down under our weight. You would be too heavy and if you didn't burst the tires, you would bend the wheels most likely," I explained apologetically.

"Oh, I would really like to do that. I think I could do that!" I could see he was really disappointed.

"Well, let me think about it for a few days. They used to make the tires solid rubber and they would probably hold you. They don't make them like that anymore because they are too heavy. But let me think about it a while and maybe I could come up with something."

A few days later, I saw him from the window of the house walking around her bike, inspecting it. I was scared he would damage it and leave me to come up with some explanation to have to tell my sis. I reminded him that he was too heavy and he asked me if I had come up with any way he could do this. I had to tell him I had not found a way that he could try it. He was disappointed.

Since he was looking for new adventures, it wasn't long before he found an avenue of expression. Pop complained about finding the big mare's halter on the floor. He brought it up to me more as a curiosity than an accusation because he knew I was good about putting the tack away.

But, one afternoon I heard the mare screaming and kicking and carrying on in her stall. She was trying to climb the walls and hollering for help. The horses had become somewhat accustomed to having Sasquatch around and only acted nervous, but they were never pressed to get too close, either.

Animals are not fooled by this 'realities' illusion. We only assume animals partake in our cultural interpretations of reality. They instead focus on what is actually there, regardless of how it registers to the eye, so they often see things and react to things that we cancel out as "not real". Therefore the mare was not fooled by Teluke's invisibility.

I ran in and flew over the feed window into her stall tripping on something in the corner before landing. It was Teluke crouching down, frightened that someone had come in. He flew out the same way I entered as it dawned on me what was going on. I called out an apology and picked up the halter laying in the sawdust. I felt bad about frightening him.

He had jumped up into the hayloft as I approached him. Teleel was up there also.

"May I talk to you for a minute?" I asked. I always tried to be as polite as possible to them because it was easy to make mistakes due to our cultural difference.

"Pop found the halter out in the isle the other day as I found this one in the stall. We always put them up when we are done, so if he keeps finding them lying around, he might think someone is trying to steal one of the horses, or start blaming me for not putting things away. If he believes someone is trying to steal one of the horses he will tighten things up around here and make things more difficult for us. Horse stealing is pretty serious to a horse owner.

"Also, you need to be careful being in the stall with a frightened horse. Even I wouldn't get in a stall with a horse that was terrified of me. It is too easy to get hurt!"

"I thought it would be safer in there!" Teluke replied as he slid down to me.

"No, not really. The horse is cornered and knows she can't get away, which makes her more nervous and defensive. They can kick real hard with their back legs and it is really easy to get pinned against the wall and hurt. Out in the open, if you get kicked, your body has room to be pushed away from her foot. You would get hurt, but not as bad as you would if you had a wall holding you there so the foot can go deeper into your body." I demonstrated with my fist. "It is also easier to get your bare feet stepped on. They are real heavy because all that weight is pressing down on four small points, their feet. That is why we wear boots around horses. They can break bones really easy. I wouldn't want you to get hurt."

"No, I wouldn't want broken bones," he said, concerned.

I went on. "I can make things easier for both of us if you will let me help you," I said, hoping he would agree.

"Oh, that is all right. She is afraid of me anyway," he said kindly.

"Well, that's a good reason we should go on with this. Horses are by nature afraid of everything because they know they are prey. You work to get a horse not to be afraid of anything. That is a valuable horse, because it is a horse you can use. If a horse is afraid of something, then that is what you work on today. I have a few tricks to get around her fears." Anxiously excusing myself, I ran into the house for something.

I brought out some Vick's salve and let them smell it. In surprise, they threw their heads back grimacing. They didn't like it. I took a strong whiff explaining that I like the smell because I am used to it.

I explained that I would put this on the horse's nostrils to confuse her sense of smell. She would not be able to smell them then. Then, I said I would also blindfold her as well.

Technically one would think this shouldn't work since the Sasquatch was invisible anyway and the horse wasn't seeing them with her eyes. But what it actually did was draw her attention away from her sixth sense and onto her eyesight which distracted her attention, telling her body "You can't see anymore." So in effect she stopped looking.

"What is blindfold?" Teluke asked.

"It will make her so she can't see," I said absently.

"No! I don't want you to hurt her eyes! You people are mean!" he exclaimed looking at Teleel, who agreed with him.

"Oh! I'm not going to injure her! I won't hurt her! I love our horses! I will just cover her eyes up so she can't see, and then I will uncover them so she will see again!" I demonstrated by cupping my hands over my eyes.

I had them stand in the barn doorway while I took the mare into the paddock from her stall. I put the Vicks on her nose right away and took my flannel shirt off that I wore over my blouse, draping it over her eyes. She stood motionless as Teluke approached her side. He wanted to pet her for a while first, so I asked if he thought his wife would also like to feel her. They oooohed and aaaahed at her soft coat, while I watched Teluke's hairy hand trace down the mare's side. Teleel returned to the doorway where she and the baby in her arms observed from a safe distance.

It was a thrill for me to be this close to Teluke. Invisible or not, he was sensational! It was endearing to me to progress in any way with the relationship. He had grown patient with me making mistakes with eye contact with him, but it was a whole different story if his wife and child were there. He would not tolerate any nonsense with her. No mistakes! No talking, and no looking at her directly. It frightened her and he was extremely protective of them.

As a rule, I was not allowed the freedom to touch him. I was still not above reproach. So it was my assumed pleasure to offer him a leg up, which meant physical contact.

"Are you sure? I'm heavy!" Teluke said, concerned.

I had done it a million times including for my own husband. So a dusty footprint rose off the ground and stuck to my pant leg that I held out for a step up. Immediately I began to holler! I could feel the bones crushing as if they were going to implode. It felt like a truck had come to rest on it! I seriously feared it was about to snap any moment. I knew he would be heavy, but I wasn't prepared for him to put his full weight on it like a step, but to just use it for momentum.

"Get up! Get up!" I yelled. The mare's back bowed way down and I worried for her. He asked me if I was all right and I shook my leg out, relieved it was over and that my leg wasn't broken. I was very annoyed from the pain and told him he had taken too long getting up. How easy it is to forget just how void complete ignorance is.

As he straddled her, I became aware of his nakedness and giggled. "I forgot you are naked. You are going to be picking horse hair out of your butt for a while. But then, that may not be the problem for you that it would be for us."

He chuckled at this, seeing the humor in it. I told him that if his wife wanted to ride I would get her a blanket to sit on because women have a different situation down there than men do.

It wasn't often that I was inches away from him. As my nose was at his knee I could get a whiff of the clean skunky odor of him, reaffirming to my senses the reality of it all. Scent is one material thing that can cross dimensions easily. Though diminished a great deal when invisible, their scent can still be detected but is no where near the strength that overpowers the nose when visible and in the same dimension as ourselves.

I happen to be one of the rare people who enjoy musky scents. I love nothing more than the stink of a rank old billy goat, or a mild skunk, which in this case wasn't a heavy odor and was quite tolerable to me.

I explained that he needed to hang on with his muscles from the knee up to the thigh. As I did so, I took privilege of my position as instructor, and touched the points of his leg. It startled him and he almost corrected me when I intercepted it, confirming the importance that he clearly understand for his safety. Smiling inside, I explained as I touched his calf as well, that holding on from the knee down would make the horse go faster and excite her.

I thoroughly relished the freedom of my position. I was, after all, keeping him safe. I was privately thrilled to the bone to be able to touch him. There was warmth in his invisible leg. It felt soft and meaty, not at all hard and muscular as I had expected. His hair was as soft and silky as an Irish Setter's. I was on high! It was as real as you or me. If I had closed my eyes I wouldn't have known by the feel that he was invisible!

I asked if he was ready and took the blindfold off the mare. She perked up and he grabbed for balance. I led her a few steps and then gave Teluke her head. She was a calm horse, one that I had given lessons on before. But again, it is easy to forget this degree of inexperience, especially in an adult.

From our earliest days we are balanced on bicycles, swings, fences, ponies. Most every adult has had some experience with balancing without the feet. It is a rare thing to come across someone who has never been off the ground at all. He said the most balancing he had ever done was walking across logs.

The mare stepped out a few yards and he grabbed for his balance hugging her with his legs, knee down, which made her pick up her speed. He fell heavily with an audible thud and a cloud of dust against the rail. The mare bolted from him once she could see what he was. Teleel and I started to run towards him at the same time, but he yelled angrily at us to stay back.

I saw in his fall that he didn't have experience in falling either. It looked like it smarted some; he fell hard. I asked if he was all right and he said yes. I caught the mare up and asked if he wanted to try again, but he said he thought it might be more fun just to watch us ride from now on. I chuckled good naturedly and told him that we have a saying that "you aren't a cowboy until you've fallen off a dozen times." But he wouldn't get back on. He quit trying to prove himself after that.

I had noticed his musk scent several times, and I asked why he smells that way. He said he didn't know, but "all men do!" he said.

"Don't women smell that way?" I asked. He said no. He said the women don't mind it at all. I recognized that this is also the case with some animals as well and I was glad for Teleel that she didn't share this attribute.

Summer was getting on and one evening I had my girlfriend Nan over for a game of horseback tag. We teased and talked dirty, laughing at each other. I climbed into an empty stall to take a whiz when it dawned on my conscious mind that someone was in there with me crouching under the feed window. I had my pants at half-mast when I realized it and let out a holler!

I heard him chuckle. My conscious mind was pretty much left ignorant when someone was around, but my Second Attention told him, "Excuse me! I didn't know this stall was being used!"

I climbed back out laughing and told Nan I would try another stall, that someone was using that one already. She laughed because nothing we were saying had to make any sense anyway and so she accepted it.

After a while, Nan was heading towards the sliding door to the paddock to clean out a brush where, apparently, Teluke had placed himself between the door and feed barrels, against the wall. As she approached, he got skittish and bolted out the door, banging the feed barrels and door with a commotion. Nan cussed and said, "Somebody was just in here!"

She said she saw his foot falls leave clouds of dust trailing into the paddock and that as he ran she saw the dusty soles of his feet as he trotted away.

Because of her presence, I had to be as blind as she was to his presence in that dimension in order to protect Teluke. He had begun to take advantage of this and made a game of it. I simply didn't know what to make of her claim.

Shortly afterward, I was standing with my back to the feed barrels, my left side to the door, when a gentle but firm, warm hand was placed - with some pressure I might add - on my right shoulder. I looked at my shoulder and saw nothing, whirled around and saw no one standing behind me, whirled some more and faced the door. My eyes and conscious mind saw nothing unusual. But way back on my subconscious mind I saw a boyish rogue in the middle of the paddock, bent part way over with his hand over his mouth to keep from laughing out loud as he again swung his leg behind him, showing his good sport attitude.

On the conscious level I was pretty scared. I had to fully participate in ignorance. I wasn't just pretending, I was scared to death. All I could figure was that it must be some demon who could do such a thing so realistically. It never dawned on me to examine what was felt inside on the touch - nothing grabbing me or hurting me. It was warm, gentle and firm, like the hand of a friend.

Early into the relationship, he had seemed hurt that I ignored him so completely when others were around and I had to explain to him that "These people have two ways of seeing. One way, the way they generally live each day, is just about completely blind and deaf to your world. They don't see or hear anything. Just once in a while they may get a glimpse into your world and it scares them.

"There are a few of us that can, and willingly do, see into your world with little or no fear. I am one of them. But I am supposed to keep you a secret. It is too easy to make a mistake and reveal your presence when others are around. So I purposely let myself be blind and deaf like they are to protect you! I simply didn't allow myself to acknowledge that I saw you last night. I wasn't aware of you."

He didn't believe or really understand why someone would choose to be blind and I told him that they are too afraid of what they see, so they shut down. Although he often was more oblivious to his invisibility than not, he had taken it as an opportunity to pull pranks on us.

Instinctively Teluke was extremely flighty. Any loud sudden noise would send him off in fear. One Saturday morning I was out in the paddock brushing my mare as Pop unloaded grain in the barn.  I had previously leaned a heavy 10 foot board against the wall near the barrels.

Teluke was outside with me talking when the board fell onto the barrels tipping them over and making a great noise.  Teluke bolted, yelling for me to run also, but I chuckled and continued my work.  When things quieted down, he came back cautiously.

"Why didn't you run?  You never run!  Didn't you hear that?" He was all wide-eyed and boyish.

"Yes, I heard it," I answered.

"Weren't you afraid?" he asked me, astonished.

"No, I wasn't afraid.  It startled me and made my body jump, but I wasn't afraid."

He asked me why not.  He seemed overwhelmingly curious and fascinated with me.

"Because I knew what that sound was and it wasn't something that would hurt me."  I realized that he was seeing things with a very ancient perception.  I seemed to understand exactly where he was coming from in his comprehension and felt great love and compassion for him.

"You are the bravest person I know!" He seemed awestruck by all the newness in his life and this strange female who wasn't afraid. The first day he ever telepathed to me, he asked me if I was a female or a male because he saw how I rode and worked right alongside the men, which led me to explain the liberated woman I am, and that men should not have all the fun.

I told him that inside each of us was both a man and a woman, to which he insisted he was all man.  He felt I should be afraid of being hurt, but I pointed out that men as well get hurt all the time and we heal. I pointed out that one judges the risks involved and decides whether they are willing to make that risk or not.

As we stood in the paddock that morning, I was again seeing the little boy emanating from his person.

"No, I am not brave at all!" I said.

"Yes, you are!"

"No, I am just as afraid as you are. Sometimes I am so afraid that I don't know if I can go on and live another day. Sometimes I feel I am too scared to go on. But, I have to be here and I don't like fear. Fear stops me from what I want to do. It interrupts my life." I thought about what this had to do with this situation.

"Have you ever been hurt by a noise?" I asked.

"No," he replied.

"That's right! Usually the noise isn't what is harmful. It's what is making the noise. I am familiar with the sound of the feed barrels and I know the feed barrels aren't going to hurt me," I went on. "When you hear a noise, try to find out what is making the noise and remember it. Is it a man banging buckets together? Or something falling? Or a car backfiring? Or a gun?"

"Most noises aren't directed at us. A sound can, however, be a warning that something might happen. A car squealing tires may mean trouble for me if I am in the street. But, if I am in the yard it probably doesn't, especially if I am not close to the road. But I will look up to see if he has lost control of the car or is just smarting off, and then I decide if I am safe or should run out of the way."

I continued, "Sometimes it is best not to run when you are afraid. An example is if a horse gets its foot caught in a fence. If he lets fear have control of his body, he will rip his leg all up, maybe kill himself in the long run. But, if the horse has been taught not to panic at times like that, he will wait patiently, until help comes and save his leg in doing so."

Teluke was placing himself in the situation. "I would not wait for someone to find me. Your people would shoot me!"

"Well, this is true! You must look at the situation and decide what would be safe for you. Are the chances greater of being found by one of my people with a gun, or one of your own coming to help you?

The fear and losing control of yourself will most often be where the harm comes in. I work to get rid of fear because fear stops me from doing things I want to do. So I look at what is going on and decide if fear is necessary or not. It usually isn't.

Like when you ran out of the barn the other night when Nan and I were out there. You gave yourself away when you let fear control you. Had you realized she could not see you and that she was walking to the door, not to you, you could have stayed put and nobody would have known you were there! Instead, you bolted and knocked the barrels and door, giving yourself away. See?"

He seemed to understand well. It seemed apparent that his people have just basic knowledge and instinct without the exercise of rationalizing or thinking things through. I suggested that rather than run all the time when he was around us and hears a noise, to look to see what our reaction is first. If we aren't running then he probably won't need to either. But if we run, it is time to look for cover.

It seemed to make sense to him because I began to notice him look at me when a noise would startle him. I would patiently tell him it was okay.

I purposely spent time alone in the barn with my mare to create the opportunity for Teluke to come up. He had been talking with me when he blurted out, "I have to go!"

I looked at him curiously as he ran outside and around the corner rather than straight back to the woods. I followed him outside to see what has up, only to be embarrassed by the physical sight of seeing a stream of urine forming out of no where, spattering the dust in the paddock. I apologized and backed away around the corner again. When he came back inside, we resumed talking.

On another occasion though, Pop was redoing the foundation of an old section of the barn near where Teluke and I were standing inside. Normally, Pop chose to remain completely ignorant of what was going on with me and the Sasquatch and Star People. But he was relaxed and that's when we're "opened" to this other world.

So it was by mistake that he picked up our telepathic conversation and stuck his head out of the stall.

"What'd you say?" he yelled. What his Second Attention saw shocked him and he telepathed, "Oh, it's him! I don't want anything to do with it!" While verbally he laughed, sort of embarrassed, and said "Oh! I thought you said something." He then made himself scarce to our presence while Teluke and I conversed. He wouldn't acknowledge the information on the conscious level that was translated from his Second Attention.

Surprised by this, I said that I hadn't said anything, upon which he withdrew and Teluke and I continued talking.

Pop was stabilizing the foundation in a stall and I was concerned about the barn collapsing, when a piece of wood snapped sharply and the barn creaked. Teluke shot a glance of surprise at me as I studied the situation and decided we might best just move on out of there, just in case, and hot-footed it into the corral.

When we were outside and nothing happened, I laughed and said, "See? Even this time it wasn't necessary. We didn't need to run. But there was a chance the barn could come down and I didn't know how big of a chance, so it was best we got out of the way to be on the safe side of things." We went back inside.

He was quite intelligent and worked to eliminate his fears. He took instructions easily and learned fast. He just didn't seem real capable of producing new thought on his own.

However, if I suggested something, it was then within his reach to apply it. He was a wonderful student! A blank computer waiting to be programmed with positive things!

There were times though that I wondered just how smart it was of me to be interfering with, what appeared to be a successful way of living, such as his people have. Their extremely healthy bodies were the result. But Zanna told me I was supposed to teach him all that I could.

So that was how I came to be standing in the shed row with my guitar.

"Female, what is that you are doing?" came his thoughts from the woods one morning.

I am playing a guitar. Want to try it?" I baited him.

He came right up and watched as I played a few songs. He really liked it and said it was beautiful, as his eyes lit up. He wanted to know if he could try it, and I readily obliged him.

As I handed him the guitar I explained not to pluck the strings out away from the box because the strings were old and could break, which, as anyone who plays a stringed instrument knows, can be very painful, if not dangerous, to those near.

My guitar was seemingly hanging in mid-air strumming itself and as his awkward arms embraced it, it bobbed and moved strangely about. He was afraid he might break it because of what I had told him about the strings.

Although I explained that the strings weren't important because I could get more and that I just didn't want him to get hurt, he only tried it for about a minute before insisting I take it back.

He asked me what I was doing with my voice and I explained singing. He thought this was very peculiar and said we sure do strange things with our bodies!

# CHAPTER THIRTEEN

## An All New You

### (Or, a New Light on the Subject)

"...and the GUARDIAN of the gate stood ready for me

half way across the bridge. His eyes were huge and reflected

from

within themselves and I knew it was his purring that filled

me

and encouraged me to take heart when I felt faint..."

T ELUKE WAS COMING UP TO the barn every day. I offered as much time as possible for these occasions, but he usually limited it to roughly an hour in late morning and an hour in the evening. If others were around I didn't get to reward myself with consciousness of him.

My Mom-in-law had an Avon showing with one of the ladies from the saddle club and offered to buy me something if I found something I liked. Zanna, as she often does, was observing things through my eyes and consciousness and pointed out a perfume cream she wanted me to try out on Teluke so he would "show himself".

We were in the paddock one morning when he got a whiff of it. He sniffed the air trying to determine its source.

"That's coming from you!" he said in amazement. "It smells like ..." he groped for the word and I telepathically saw him in a field smelling flowers.

"Flowers?" I filled in for him. "It's called Roses, Roses, Roses!"

"It smells good! How do you smell that way? You always smell good!" He had that surprised little boy look again.

"We call it perfume. I like this because it smells like real flowers. Roses are one of the most fragrant flowers there are!"

I went about my chores and he became playful. He darted around the paddock acting from instinct with what his body felt like doing. It appeared to be an instinctive showing off his prowess as a child might do without realizing they were showing off.

I watched for a moment, amused, then left the barn doorway. Teluke called me back. "Don't leave! Watch me!" he said.

"What are you doing?" I asked, so I would understand.

"I'm showing you how I hunt!" His voice was rather pitiful and pleading.

I watched then and saw that he was crouching, stalking, rushing and hiding and then went in for the kill with what I presume was an imaginary spear or rock.

Running out of room in the paddock, I heard him muse to himself that he runs a long way as he trotted back and forth, then ran in place a moment before throwing his non existent weapon. Then he stood over his imaginary kill triumphantly, raising his fists and shouting a primal scream for all the mountains and meadows to take notice of his greatness.

"You did that very well!" I praised him though I loathe any kind of killing. "What animal did you kill?"

"I didn't kill any animal!" he said in surprise.

"I mean, what did you pretend to kill?"

"A deer," he responded.

I acknowledged his deed, but couldn't help restate that I had a hard time appreciating murder. Not wanting to spoil his theatrics though, I reaffirmed that he did well with it!

I went over to clean out a brush and he dashed up to me and stood extremely close. His chest touched my elbow. I realized he was making contact with <u>me</u>. He was flirting. I reached up and placed my hand squarely on his chest and he fell away.

"Don't touch me!" He hadn't liked it at all.

"Then don't stand so close!" I told him smiling, and turned to go to the barn. But I bumped into him on the other side. I laughed, accepting it as my fault and excused myself. I went to enter the barn but he blocked me again. I knew this game and took it up, faking a dodge and darted past him on into the barn. I kept my eyes to the ground, purposely avoiding eye contact. He blocked me again and I wouldn't look at him. I just knew not to! I laughed and said, "What are you doing?"

"I want you to look at me!" he said coolly.

"I can't help but look at you! I can't see anything else!" I giggled at the silliness of his statement.

I struggled to get passed him but as my ribs hit his outstretched arms it was like bashing them against hard metal bars. It hurt me. We ended up against the feed barrels. I was trapped. I was feeling insecure and didn't know if this was a game or not anymore. I was becoming frightened.

"I want you to look at my eyes!" he said firmly.

I rolled around and leaned over the barrels to avoid it. "No! I'm not gonna look at you! I know what you're going to do to me! I won't look at your eyes!"

We were working in the Second Attention and I was drawing from old knowledge from past lives, some of which I presently have conscious memory of.

"**Look at me!**" he ordered.

"No," I squeaked out. I felt like a little child. "Let me go, or I'll **touch you!**" I turned around, brandishing my hands like almighty weapons.

His voice was a warning that erased any though of advancing and totally disarmed or rather in this case, "dis-handed" me completely.

"If you touch me, I will kill you. Don't do it. I am not going to let you go until you look at me!"

I knew I could not escape his swift movements or his strength. I didn't know if I was in trouble or not. I checked in with Zanna on the star ship for her opinion. She resignedly said I should look at him then.

I felt so betrayed by her! I had reached out to her for help and she seemed to dismiss me, telling me to submit to the situation. After all, this was her fault, getting me into this mess in the first place by having me buy that perfumed cream!

I turned around slowly and cautiously looked into his eyes and passed out immediately. When I came to, Teluke was kneeling over me on the cold damp earth of the barn floor.

"How long was I out?" I asked, confused.

"You just went down. Are you all right? I thought I killed you!" he asked sweetly. His voice was genuinely concerned and I could see it in his face.

"Yeah! What was that?" What I had seen was **so awesome** that it was horrendous to my physical body and I passed out to protect myself. The pupils of his eyes had become star shaped holes from which burst forth a brilliant white light. I was not at all afraid now. But I had never seen anything like that before anywhere, while in this body, this life.

"That was me! Are you afraid of me now?"

My thoughts raced. "Why? Are you gonna hurt me? Do I have reason to be afraid of you?" I wondered.

"No, I'm not going to hurt you," his voice was serious.

"You're still you, aren't you?  Are you any more dangerous now that I have seen you?"  I was speaking of the entity I had momentarily seen.

"Yes, I'm still me." He shook his head "no", that he wasn't any more dangerous.

"Are you sure you're a human being?" There is a great deal that I don't know, but I believe that with God all things are possible.  I have had some awesome and unexpected discoveries in my short life, so I do not draw full conclusions, that is... shutting the door to new possibilities.

"Yes, I <u>am human</u>!" He was adamant and secure in his words in a way that assured me that he was not lying.  He spoke words as truth.  I may not always know when I am being lied to, but I do know truth when I hear it.  It rings true.

I asked why he did that and he said he wanted to show himself to me.  He said that he thought it would frighten me, though.

"Did you do this to frighten me?"  I was appalled at the thought.

"No," he assured me kindly.  I could see apprehension in his eyes as to whether I would believe him or not.

"May I see you again?" I inquired.

"You want to see me again?  You just keep surprising me! You are not afraid of **anything**! Yes! I will show you!" His expression was excitement, great surprise and joy.

He went across the aisle-way and I began to follow, but he told me to stay where I was.  He stood against the wall and came out from the eyes as a brilliant white light and appeared in form.  His gorilla body stood in a daze behind him and I chuckled at its glazed expression.

I was startled and took hold of myself, preparing for what I was about to lay my eyes on. Not fully knowing what to expect, having passed out the first time, I shielded my eyes, peered through my fingers and told him to tell me when he was out.

Manifesting before me towered something I had never before seen or expected to see! As his eyes began to illuminate, he came out as a column of cloud that intensified in density until it was solid in brilliant form and seemed to step down into full manifestation. I could hear his garments rustle with his movements.

"OK, you can look now!" he said. His mouth did not move as he spoke. "I can't believe you're not afraid of me!"

I laughed. "My family tells me the same thing, that I always surprise them. I've told you, I'm not like other people. I love you! I know what I feel and what I feel from you is not evil or negative energy! I am not fooled by outer appearances like other people are. You are still you no matter what form you take on. I don't care what you look like! I know what I feel in my heart, and what I feel is good! You are a pure being! You really are a higher being!"

His expression was of delight that I saw this.

"I'm a Kachina!" he told me joyously. I had not heard that word before, but liked it immediately.

I cannot conclude just what makes us human beings. The Star People are human, yet completely different in many ways from us, like human blanks. Who knows what the higher self looks like anyway! He certainly was communicating to me intelligently. That at least has to be the basis of something human. He was flesh and blood as well.

He towered maybe eight to ten feet tall. His eyes radiated an intense white light. His head was cylindrical shaped and had three beautiful white spiraled horns, one on each side of the top and one at the rear. When his head moved, or any part of him, it intensified the reality to me and was startling to my body.

He was bare-chested and had a bandolier across his left shoulder that ran to his right hip. He had on a kilt that I believe was white, the bandolier I recall being red. His legs were white and he wore rust colored Navaho style moccasins with white soles.

There was a small pouch at the waist that he said had medicine in it. His mouth was a straight red line that looked like it was painted on rather than a useful mechanism. The face I was having a little difficulty relating to.

"You have three horns! I didn't know anything had three horns!" I exclaimed. "Do you use them as weapons? It looks like it might be fun to have horns!"

He acknowledged the three horns and said they don't usually use them except in mock battles and ceremonies.

"May I touch them?" I asked enthusiastically.

"Yes," he said and bent over for me to touch them. They were smooth and warm and very dense, physical horns.

"Do the females have horns, too?"

"Yes, we all do."

"Even the baby?"

"Not yet, but she will get them soon," he said.

"Your mouth doesn't look real. Is it painted on?" My childlike innocence always got me to ask pertinent questions.

"It's real," he said and pulled it at the corner a bit.

"Do you have teeth? What do you eat?" I asked.

"We don't have teeth. We eat food that you wouldn't understand. It is just in the other world. It's good!" he complied willingly.

"Why do you have clothes on this body? You sure give me a hard time about my wearing clothes!"

Looking at them more thoroughly I asked, "What are they made of?" I didn't recognize the material.

"It's something we make. I don't know how to describe it to you."

"You make it yourself?" I was surprised he was so technologically advanced. He acknowledged it with a smile.

"Does Teleel look like this, too? Do all of you look like this?"

"Yes," he smiled again. He said the baby would get her horns soon now.

"You have three bodies!" It was as much of a question as a statement.

"No, we only have two," he assured me.

"No, you don't! You have three! How come you have three when we only have two! You have this one, that one (pointing to his glazed gorilla body standing there behind him), and the one that astral projects and looks like the gorilla!" I explained.

He was somewhat puzzled to see this point and recognize the truth of it. He didn't know why he had three. He had never thought about it like that.

"Why doesn't this body look like that one?" I asked.

"We like this body better. We don't really like that one. Some man, a long time ago, tried to make us a better one. It was a big mistake." He shook his head at the thought. He seemed to shudder inside. "It didn't turn out good at all!"

"What happened to it? Can you show me?" I asked inquisitively.

He shook his head no. "I didn't see it myself. It was a long time ago. Someone showed me. I won't show you. It was horrible. We don't show the females. It wasn't made right at all. He didn't know if he should kill it or not. They didn't even know if it was alive or not!" He seemed to be sick inside.

"What happened to it?"

"It died."

"Why?" I asked.

"He didn't know how to feed it," he looked at me thoughtfully. "He didn't know where the mouth was. It was a blessing when it died. The man can't come back here anymore, he's being punished." Then he added in reflection and a twinkle of amusement, "Well, he can, but he doesn't think he can. He thinks he should be punished." His smile belayed his warm telepathic feelings.

"Well! I like the gorilla body just fine!" I told him, changing the subject to lighten things again.

"But this body is even faster! Watch and I'll show you!" the sporty rogue still emanated from his personality.

I looked up at his new form and he told me not to watch him because he was too fast and I would miss it. He told me to look out in the pasture.

When I looked out the barn door, I saw him standing out there waving at me!

"Here I come again!" he said, and instantly stood beside me again.

"Wow! That was neat!" I was appropriately impressed.

I had seen his silver cord strung out between his gorilla body and his new body. I asked him what would happen if someone tried to pass between them, interfering with the cord. He said he was too quick and would not let it happen. He said he didn't really know about that.

There was some reason that evades me at the present that he wanted me to go out into the pasture with him. He wanted to show me something else. He said he would race me, but I said that it wouldn't be any fun to race because I was too slow. I asked him to walk with me. He didn't walk but floated effortlessly across the paddock beside me. It looked painfully slow for him. I told him regretfully, that I had to crawl under the railing, as he passed right through it. I don't recall what took place in the pasture.

Back inside the barn, he told me he had wanted to show himself to me. He said that he and his mate do "this" (become Kachinas) when they "join". They go into each other.

I had known instinctively that looking at him would be to momentarily absorb into him and so I wouldn't do this. I passed out to stop it.

Teleel then called him back to the woods to remind him that he was already mated and when he returned to me, he immediately kept his place. He was devoted to Teleel and had just gotten carried away in the present moment. He said they had not been married long and he had "forgotten".

At the present time, as an adopted member of the Eagle Clan of Miami Indians, I now understand that what I saw in Teluke's transformation was a Kachina from the Native American cultures. This is a revered and holy spiritual being that is a keeper of some power of nature. They are the caretakers of the earth.

It was startling to see him this way, but to add movement to this unique personage was even more awesome. I got used to it quickly though.

On the First Attention, I was confused as to why I had passed out. Being concerned, I went on in the house when Teluke and I parted. I told Mom that I had blanked out for an instant. Everything that happened on the Second Attention was quietly stored away.

We enjoyed our time together immensely from that point, and looked forward to our time together. We each had a whole new world to explore.

The next time he made a remark about my clothes, I confronted him with the fact that he wore them too, and had no right to criticize me for it, which he flat out denied!

Zanna, being aware of our interaction, cautioned me against exposing this information to him because he was not aware of his Kachina body in the conscious state.

# Chapter Fourteen

## Grow Where You Are Planted

*"...when corn stalks lick the arms and legs*

*and birds of night will sing*

*and spicy odors from the earth*

*that rising heat will bring..."*

W E PLAYED AROUND WITH THE idea of "time". I counted out a second for him and a minute. Then I explained when time was essential and when it was used loosely as an expression. I had run into the house once telling him I would be just a minute. I came back in about three or four minutes and he tried to tell me I had lied. I explained that I had said "just a minute" and not "just one minute". He was beginning to understand how communication within our people causes misunderstandings between he and I.

I told him that if I say, "I am going in to change my clothes into something cooler and I will only be a second," that it was up to him to know it will take me longer than a second to even get into the house. But if I was gone for an hour or more and left him standing out here waiting for me, then he would be justified to be mad at me and I would be at fault.

We were having fun together. I believe I may have learned more than he did, because the gifts that he was giving me were, at least in my perception, far more valuable. I was learning what it takes to be truly pure and innocent and free. I got to see childlike, naked, unadulterated innocence of heart! The way God must have intended for us to remain. I could only assume this is how we must have been before we fell in the Garden of Eden. It was something I dearly hoped one day to return to! We are so judgmental about everything that we complicate our lives into every form of illness.

One Monday morning I was out in the barn lot when I heard Teluke's solemn voice come up to me from the woods into my head.

"I am sorry about what happened," his voice was soft and respectful.

"Sorry about what?" I was puzzled. Had he done something? Compassion filled me for the remorse in his tone.

"About somebody dying," he said sorrowfully.

"Dying? Who died?" I was surprised.

"Didn't somebody die?" he was surprised.

"No," I said. "Why would you think that?"

He explained, "Well, it was so quiet up at your place we couldn't figure out why! My wife and I both thought somebody must have died!"

I laughed. "OOH, NO! We had a wonderful time this weekend! We took the horses to Brown County to trail ride. It was wonderful!"

He asked me about it.

"We put the horses in the trailer and go where there are lots of trees and meadows and hills to ride in. We sleep outside each night under the stars and breathe fresh air! I love it! It's so healing to me! I wish I could live outdoors! It sounds like you missed me, huh?" I could have sworn I heard Teleel giggle.

Later on, he broke the bottom rail in the paddock, about knee high from the ground, rushing back to the woods for an emergency. The baby had hurt herself on a stick. Teluke apologized for the broken board and I told him Pop would just think one of the horses had kicked it. I was glad the baby was all right.

To see the Sasquatch run is remarkable. It is like following a lightning bolt with your eye. I had the opportunity to see this several times. The bottom half of him was a blur. I can't imagine it's possible to do what it would take to cause this effect, both the speed and the blur. It is hard to imagine anyone picking their feet up and putting them down that fast. But I asked him once to slow it down enough for me to see his legs, and sure enough, he was doing just that! He was never out of breath more than a few extra puffs of air would take care of. His stamina was that of a vibrant 10-year-old!

We had fun exploring all kinds of things together. He had asked me what it was that my mate's father wears on his face. I explained that they were glasses we use to help people who have poor eyesight, to better see. I told him that I wear them also and went to retrieve mine from the pickup. I could just see my hairy friend in horn-rimmed glasses. I laughed at the thought.

I handed them to him and told him not to put them on because the arms don't bend that far out. I showed him that he could look through them backwards. He scrunched up his face and peered out into the pasture. He was gentle with my things and respected my belongings. He was as kind and considerate as anyone I have ever met.

He was still very protective of his family, but when it was just he and I, I savored every moment. He was a special very magical friend to have. In awe one afternoon, I told him he was like having a best friend and a favorite pet all in one. He didn't like me saying that, and stated again he was not an animal!

Even though we seemed to get along, he remained leery and distrustful. I was not allowed to touch him freely and when I began offering them food, he questioned me each time if I had poisoned it.

This truly hurt me to the quick. I could not comprehend that he would think such a thing of me when I loved them so. It seemed to me that he should automatically sense this strong devotion I had for them. But he explained that my people do these kinds of things to his people. He wasn't trying to be offensive about it, just being careful. I could appreciate that.

I once was leaving for the weekend to visit my parents in Speedway and went out to let Teluke know I would be gone a while. He asked me if he could go along so he could meet my Mother. I considered the complications.

"Well, I don't really like taking you so far away from here. It's about an hour drive from here, and if you got scared, there would be no woods for you to run to. I know you would be welcome in their home, my Mom would just love you! But I am afraid you may get scared and need to run!"

"I would call the ship and they would come for me," he said.

"What if they didn't come or couldn't come right away?" I asked. That mode of escape seemed pretty chancy to me.

"They always come!" he pleaded.

"Could you ride in the truck for an hour?"

"Yes, I could do that," he assured me. He really wanted to meet her!

"Well, I'm going to be gone for two nights. Would you be able to live with us and stay in the house that long?" I would need to introduce the toilet and other things to them.

"No," he said resignedly. "I would not want to be gone that long."

"Well, that's too bad. I know my Mother would really like you. She is a lot like me that way. She doesn't judge people by their differences. Maybe some other time, Ok?" I was sorry to leave them behind.

I told my Mother that I almost brought out a very special friend who wanted to meet her. She smiled and told me my friends were always welcome there. She said she like meeting my friends. I told her that he was an invisable being and lived in the woods. She smiled condescendingly at what she thought was my "wonderful imagination" and let it go.

Teluke and I shared as much about our two very different worlds as possible with each other. I walked into the barn once with a Faygo pop and he asked me if he could see it.

Seeing him with my Second Attention and the bottle with my regular sight, I didn't miss a beat. When I handed him the bottle, it switched dimensions and disappeared from visual sight, and appeared to me on the Second Attention. He examined the bottle and said he always wondered what those were. He had seen them lying in the woods at times. He asked if he could try it and I said "sure." He didn't care for it and handed it back to me.

Another time I walked out into the field with a glass of iced tea. He wanted to know about it and I told him it was cold. He didn't know how it could be cold so I brought out a glass of ice cubes for them. They told me later that they threw them away because they were too cold.

I steadily gained his trust that I was not going to hurt them. I had proven myself enough that he was seeing in hindsight his own misconception of me. We stood in the barn one day talking about how hot it was and that I needed to take a bath. He was curious and asked how we get our water. I tried to explain it but he couldn't fathom what I meant. No one was at home right then so I offered to take him in the house to show him if he wanted.

"You know by now that I won't hurt you, don't you?" I asked.

"Well, I guess so." And since it was just he and I, he didn't have to concern himself about protecting his family.

When we went in, I made sure to prop the door open for him even though he said it wasn't necessary. I showed him the hot water explaining that it came from a water heater in the basement. He wanted to see it. I took him to the basement door and saw the old steps. I didn't know if they would hold him, so I suggested I go down and look at it for him. I went down and looked at it, leaving my mind open and sending my vision telepathically. "Can you see it?" He affirmed that he did.

I showed him the refrigerator and had him stick his hand into the freezer with mine. He was surprised. I explained that this was one of the ways we keep food to eat for winter.

I showed him the bathroom and flushed the toilet for him so he could understand. While we talked, I remembered the telephone.

"This is how we talk to people far away. Want to try it?" I encouraged him. He thought that would be interesting, so I picked up the receiver and thought for a moment who to call. My Mother!

I dialed the phone and when she answered I asked her if she would recite the Lord's Prayer for me, saying I had forgotten some of it.

"Oh! Well…. Our Father, who art in heaven…." I handed the phone to Teluke and told him that as soon as she stopped talking to give it back to me right away.

He stood there blinking his eyes thoughtfully, then handed it back to me. I thanked my Mother and hung up.

"What was that she was saying? It was nice!" he asked respectfully.

"That was the Lord's Prayer," I smiled.

"What is prayer? She used words like these but they were different. I liked it, though," he reflected.

"Prayer is when we talk to God. Do your people pray?" I asked.

"No. Well, not like that. We always do!" I got the impression that they are just in a state of constant communion with God and don't need to take time out for specific talking. I told him that the words she used were an old way of speaking. We went outside.

"I would sure like to meet her!" Teluke said.

When the in-laws returned home, they turned up their noses when they came in the house and said, "It sure smells bad in here!" and opened up all the windows to air the house out.

When I next visited my Mother, I told her that she said The Lord's Prayer that day to a Sasquatch. She looked at me strangely and said, "You keep talking about this stuff. Are you really doing this? Maybe I should pay more attention to you! I wish you had told me. I would have liked to talk to him!"

I explained that he doesn't talk like we do and dropped it. I couldn't acknowledge the truth further, so I had to just let her wonder.

As summer rolled on, Pop, Byron and I would be out road riding on the horses and sometimes would pass the Sasquatch family out meandering through the countryside looking for food. It usually scared the horses and I would caution them to be careful not to be seen. Sometimes they were right up in people's front yards, window peeping.

Before long they told me they were going to stay in this other man's barn for a while. I knew the man, as he was in our horse club. I told them I was sorry they were leaving me. But I did not own them. They were free to be where ever they felt they needed to be, I guess. It hurt me, but all I could do was help them anyway I knew how.

"That man seems to be a good person. He may be accepting of you, but he does hunt, so he has guns there. Please be careful! I love you all so much! Keep yourselves safe for me?" I asked them. "I will miss you!"

"We will miss you, too!" they said together. "But we will come visit you!"

I had seen Teluke come out of the cornfield with an armload of food once and he almost stepped out in front of a car. I begged him to be careful. I was extremely afraid that a car might honk its horn while he was in there and make him panic and run out before looking and get hit. I explained to look both ways before stepping out into the street. He figured that I thought he was stupid since I was always informing him, and he didn't appreciate it much at times. But I assured him that I was only looking out for his safety.

I was glad that they took care of themselves and that I did not have to tend to them all of the time. At the beginning I had worried so about them that if Byron and I went anywhere, I would not stay long and wanted to come right home. This was necessary though. On some really deep level Byron must have known because there was an acknowledgement. He understood and would agree willingly to leave.

One evening I was amazed when we were coming out of the Marion County fairgrounds, a good ways from the farm, and saw the family outside the grounds. Teluke had an armload of food and Teleel had the child. It scared me for their safety to be so public. I told them not to go in there because there were guns in there. He asked me why they need guns and I told him that the police make sure the bad people don't cause any trouble.

He said they had heard all the noise and it sounded like they were having fun and they wanted to get a closer look. I told them to be careful to wash the food good, in case it had poison on it from pesticides. He said he checked it and that it was clean.

The reason I was so concerned for them to be so public was because, although the eye did generally not see them, there are enough psychic people that could easily detect them.

Pop happened to be like Byron in that he was aware of them on the Second Attention but he would not acknowledge it on the conscious level, even so much as their presence being felt. They both simply ignored what they sensed and withdrew. I knew they could at times hear me telepathically converse with them, but they purposely shut off the connection to the waking conscious mind.

The food was drying up and I saw more of them. They had returned to the farm because we had more food even though that wasn't much. He said they were always hungry now because the plants weren't growing back. I told him that this is when we have the most food. He puzzled at this and I explained that we plant it so that it is ready to pick at this time. Then we save it for winter use. He really thought this was a good idea and asked why the garden food didn't come back after being picked, like wild food does and I tried to explain as best I knew about hybrid foods.

As we stood and talked, he said they didn't like the other barn. "You take good care of your horses. That other man never brushed his horses and made them stand in the dark and never let them out. They had to stand in their ..." He didn't have a name for manure.

"I know. It makes me sick to see people claim to love their animals, then treat them like that. They want the fun of riding them and won't reward them with good care. Most people don't deserve their animals. Animals are such a blessing to us. They need love and grooming and regular feeding and fresh water and sunshine just like we do! They even enjoy excitement!

And what is even worse is that animal doctors take up their profession supposedly because of their love for animals, but they charge outrageous prices and get rich with it so people refuse to spend that kind of ridiculous money and dump their animals somewhere or take them to the pound to be destroyed. Some vets will tell you, 'Maybe you can't afford to have animals then,' and that makes me mad.

Caring for our animals is our birthright! That was our purpose to be here! The doctors are the ones at fault. They will even turn away a sick or injured animal that you find, if you can't or aren't willing to pay them for fixing it."

Teleel seemed to understand me and nodded in disappointment, and Teluke agreed. He wrapped his arm around her and they seemed glad to be back home.

# CHAPTER FIFTEEN

## Surreal Encounters

*"…before me ever lies a private showing of things*

*untouchable by mortal men…"*

While Byron, like Pop, preferred to remain blissfully ignorant on the conscious level about what I was up to, being in a relaxed state tends to automatically open doors that one may prefer remain shut.

Riding horses is at times one of these relaxing exercises that opens the channels of reception to these other dimensions of reality.

And so it was that Byron, at one point, pointed out to me that there was a "ghost-like" man lying belly down with his chin on his arms, out in the hay field watching us ride and continually changing places as he came closer. Byron wasn't alarmed by it, though.

Eventually Teluke ended up lying under the railing and grabbing for the horses legs as we rode by, which caused the horses to "blow" and get disciplined. I laughed at him and told him not to scare the horses, and cause them to be reprimanded. Amused, I told him to move back a bit so he wouldn't get hurt.

Byron did come close on several occasions to an actual experience on the conscious level. One evening at dusk,when we were riding in the paddock he called me over to the rail to look at these red glowing eyes watching us. I tried to make little of it as I acknowledged it and trotted on by, but he had me halt.

"Wait a minute! Watch them! Watch till they blink! There is no body there behind them!"

I watched briefly, trying to pass it off lightly, but then I saw what he was seeing on the First Attention. It was amusing to see two pair of red glowing eyes and when they blinked there was no shadow or image there, nothing! Just pasture, the ground behind them! I found it precious to know someone was trying to be sneaky watching us and they weren't doing a very good job of hiding themselves.

They were a dead giveaway as they watched. It just struck me as humorous to see the eyes blinking and looking around. I commented that I had not seen eyes glow red like that before.

Generally, animals eyes shine yellow or green to the best of my knowledge. It made me think of some exotic animal like a hyena or something. It wasn't horrible or scary as one must imagine about "red glowing eyes!" It was just a different color of eye-shine that was not the result of reflection off of something external, but from their inner light.

I called to them verbally! "We see you," and the eyes shut and the couple got up and trotted back to the woods giggling like children. I telepathed to them that they didn't have to leave. We would not bother them. They slowed down to a walk and said "Oh, that's all right. We were through for the evening anyway. Besides, it's no fun anymore when you have been discovered."

It was wonderful to have them within range of thought to talk with. I understood that as long as I was anywhere on the farm I could touch and be touched telepathically by them. Yet, Teluke surprised me one evening when we were traveling with Byron's family a good distance away, by discussing something with me quietly as we drove along. I know presently, that telepathy is infinite..........

Knowing I was supposed to help him learn everything I could, I picked them up a watermelon one day at the store. I sliced it most of the way in half and took it out to the force field and laid it down. I told them that we find it a refreshing summer treat on hot days, and to spit out the seeds and to just eat the red stuff and stop when it begins to get white and bitter. They thanked me and came to get it. When next I spoke to them they said they didn't care that much for it because there was too much water. What can I say? I tried.

Harvest time came and it was haying time. I drove the pick-up around the field alternating loads with another truck. I sat waiting for them to fill the other truck when Teluke came up to the pick-up.

"Hi!" he stood there a moment. "Do you think I could drive the truck out here?" he asked me sheepishly.

It hadn't occurred to me to try it out here and the men wouldn't be ready for me for a while. I found it a wonderful idea!

"Yeah! That's a great idea!" I hollered.

His face beamed at my unexpected response. I jumped out and had him hop in and scoot over so I could let him see me drive to see how it's done first. Then I popped out of the truck and traded places. I sat facing him on the edge of the seat and braced myself with one arm on the dash and the other on the seat. I told him that I knew he would be able to do it if he just kept trying and not quit when he failed.

"You're a lot like me! You know that?" I asked him. He looked at me questioning the likelihood of that.

"You aren't afraid to try new things! That's how you learn! Don't give up if you fail. Just keep trying and one day you will succeed at just about whatever you try new!"

I had explained the gears and clutch and gas and brake, relying on his good memory. He started the truck. It leaped forward and died. He was disappointed and I reminded him that this is normal for everyone that tries to drive a stick shift the first time. He brightened up and tried again. Every once in awhile we would go a few yards before it died. Then he got it right and we cruised towards the fence at the back of the pasture. I cheered him on! But the fence was coming closer and I panicked, causing him to kill it. I had him let me turn the truck around so he could head down the other way then. We leaped and lurched about half way down the field and he called it quits. He said he didn't know why he was having such a hard time now when he got it right once.

I told him that it was probably his anticipation and anxiety from doing it once. I said that sometimes that makes us fail because we want it so badly. "Now, aren't you glad I made you drive the car first? I wanted you to feel good and confident in yourself. Not sad like you feel now." I paused for his acknowledgement and went on.

"See? I am taking care of you. I do know what I'm talking about sometimes. I wanted you to be able to drive! I know this is difficult for everybody and the car is a lot easier. I wanted you to be successful as much as you wanted to do it. You really did pretty good today! If you were able to practice it, I have no doubt that you would do it eventually!"

The men haying were ready for my truck and I had to leave him. He was pleased with his attempts though and for the opportunity. He thanked me warmly and returned to the woods unnoticed.

The men had noticed that the hay at the end of the field had been all trampled down and wondered how it happened. There were no herds of deer in rural New Palestine area any more than there were bear.

When I was out riding the next evening under the harvest moon at dusk, Teluke came out to the paddock. We talked about the delicious smell of new mown hay and he asked what we had been doing in the pasture. I told him that we put hay up to feed the horses during the winter. He seemed impressed with this new train of thought. Having food in the winter appealed to him a lot. I loved opening new doors of thought for him. It would be well if his people could replicate the idea with their own food somehow.

When October rolled around I had decided to have the people I worked with in Gnotobiotics, out for a Halloween party weener-roast out in the pasture. I was excited to have this opportunity for fun.

I worked all day, carrying blocks out into the pasture for the fire pit, then hay bales to sit on. Teluke asked me what I was doing and I told him I was getting ready for a party. He was apprehensive and said he had heard about those. He wanted to know if we would be drinking that stuff that makes us crazy. He worried that people would be tramping through the woods and all.

I assured him that these people were pretty decent. I explained that there were only two men I should be watchful of for that, but I would insist they follow the rules and would keep them out of the woods. It wasn't our woods to begin with. He said in a disgusted tone, that our people don't keep to our rules and he didn't believe it would go well at all.

I had come up to the woods to get firewood and he told me to stay and he would get it for me. He didn't want me in the woods. On the conscious level or First Attention, I was not always fully aware of the conversations or the interactions that took place when

I was using the Second Attention. Much of what went on was quite often a mystery to me as well.

So I found it strange to find wood lying over the fence for me. Forest debris was never a problem to clean up along the fence when we mowed hay because the fence was just out of reach of the branches so nothing fell onto our land. Our pasture was void of trees.

I spoke to Pop about this curiosity of finding wood in a pile and yet distinctly and sub-consciously knew a man was putting it over the fence for me, because he didn't want me in the woods. It was then even more affirming to my senses and conscious mind when I went up for the second load and found it there as well, because I had expected on the conscious level to need to go into the woods. I had thought I would walk around a bit while I was in there. Teluke was a bit perturbed by the second load because he needed some for winter and he felt I was using a bit more than necessary.

One piece of wood was a 10 or 15-foot limb, 8 inches or more in diameter. This was definitely not reasonable to believe it had just fallen into the pasture of its own accord.

I had gotten my yellow mare out to drag the log back for me. It wasn't a good idea to begin with because she was a hot-blooded Saddlebred. But I had prided myself in having trained her to do just about everything so it wasn't something I would not try.

The first problem I realized was getting her to enter the force field. I had forgotten that little detail. She was the one mare that was always pleased to give it a wide berth. But I finally got her within reach of the log at ropes length and had her ground tied.

That is to say she was "tied" to the ground by an imaginary tether, which I had her trained to believe was there.

I got off and tied the one end of the rope to the log and remounted. I knew not to wind the rope about the saddle horn in a way that could not be freed easily. In fact, I had planned to be able to just hold the rope with my hand and drag it behind us. But the log was apparently lodged in the ground a tad from its initial impact, plus it was quite heavy, not allowing me to proceed as planned. So the alternative was to just hook the rope over the horn for leverage and to give me a solid base from which to haul the log.

I had the mare facing the barn, away from the woods. When she felt the weight of the log on the saddle she jerked and saw it leap towards her out of the corner of her eye. She whirled around to face it. This wound the rope over the top of itself so I could not free it. She jerked backwards and the log jumped towards her, startling her even more.

Things were looking bad. I strongly advised her to go forward, but she was too afraid to be able to hear me. I kicked her and cussed her and the more she disobeyed the more the log threatened to attack her. I could not get her attention. All I needed was just enough slack, just a few inches to unwind the damn rope, but she felt it was asking too much. She was almost hysterical, ready to blow, all white eyed and lathered up.

I struggled to gain control, but it just kept the log leaping at her, frightening her more. The rope would not free itself. It was extremely frustrating because it would be so easy to unwind the rope if she would just give me the slack I needed! We danced around the field on the end of the rope until she had succeeded to tie me up royally. I was being pinched in half. Not quite the way I had hoped to get my hourglass figure! I had to get the damned rope off me!

Teluke saw I was in trouble and stepped up to the fence. "Are you all right?" he asked me, as he studied the situation.

"No! I'm not all right! She is going to kill me if I don't get this rope off me! It looks like you are going to get to see one of my people get killed after all!" I said, sarcastically.

Teluke stepped closer to the fence and started to come over it, but the mare became harder to control!

"Don't come any closer! You are scaring her more!" I said. He stood there concerned and helpless.

I saw that I was unable to turn the mare around the one way to unwind the rope off me. It just wasn't working. Something had to be done now! With no other alternative, I decided to try to work the rope up and over my head.

I stuck my arms underneath it. When I had worked it up to my shoulders, I realized that if it slipped quickly off my shoulders it would pinch my head off! The mare was constantly dancing so the rope went constantly from taught to tighter! It was one of those times when you realize your life depends on one slim chance.

My odds were not good!

From deep within my soul, I willed. I drew upon all the power in the sky as well. "I will not die! I will not let you kill me! I have it within me to overcome this. I will live."

Holding the hysterical mare in one hand and taking the rope in the other, I physically pulled the mare a few steps towards the log and flipped the rope over my head. It snapped tight with a twang.

Having done this, the rope was then wound an extra time about the horn. I knew then I had lost the battle. All this was about as much fun as I could handle.

I let the mare blow up.

We raced to the barn. All that work to avoid this very thing and here we go anyhow! A half hour of my life wasted that I will never get back again!

A horse that runs off with you in anger is relatively safe to be on. You just hold on and endure the ride. But a horse that is running in fear is running blind and will run smack into things. They just go blind with fear. I did <u>not</u> want to be here. I was positive I didn't see this on today's agenda; it was scheduled for somebody else's day, I was just sure!

My alternative was to bail off. The ground was soft and damp from a previous rain, so it wouldn't be like jumping or falling from a fast car onto pavement, I guessed. So I leaped and rolled and then horrified, I realized the rope was whizzing down my body and soon there would come a log to remove my head. It seemed one way or another my head was likely to be displaced!

Zanna telepathed to me "Roll!", which I did again, just as the log ripped off my sleeve and pant leg. I was in shock at how close I had come to losing my lid.

The mare spun around the paddock gate exploding the log when it hit the corner posts. Somehow by the grace of God, the other mares and foals who were watching from the paddock missed being struck by all the projectiles flying through the air.

I lay there dazed. "Am I alive? Yes. Anything missing?" I felt each member as I tried it out. "No, it seems to be all here. Anything broken?" That was the scary part for me. I could handle not have a part, but not broken bones. I have been known to come very close to passing out just from listening to stories about broken bones! "Doesn't seem to be anything broken!" But it all sure hurt!

Slowly I lifted myself off the ground and tried it all out. "Boy! I could have been killed! It would have been a while before Pop or Byron found me, too!" I thought to myself. As I got to my feet my Second Attention caught sight of Teluke at the end of the field, stopping mid-stride as he was heading up to help me at a run. I sent my thoughts out to him that I was okay.

I was really kind of touched that he would do this. As much as I wanted to believe he liked me, he would never admit to such a thing. He always liked to play that part down even though it was evident at times when we got along. It was better to pretend that I never saw him heading up to help me.

The results of the disaster were good, though. The wood was in nice pieces and I could handle it without bothering the men. And there were only remaining two badly shaken beings. I felt bad for the mare. She was in such terror that it took me a long time to calm her down so I could unsaddle her. There remains a deep rope burn in the saddle horn today to remind me of the affair.

# Chapter Sixteen

## In Confidence Relied

*"...wet leaves that permeate the air*

*and wind that strips the trees*

*the Autumn Angel heralding*

*the coming of the freeze."*

ALL THINGS CONSIDERED, I THINK it's safe to say we were both looking forward to the seasonal event. I had decided to come to the party as an airplane and had bought a clear plastic false face to conceal my identity. Zanna prompted me to take it out back and show Teluke.

So I carried it out and told him what I had. He wanted me to enter the force field and come closer and put it on. I turned my back to him and told him not to be afraid when I turned around. He said he wouldn't be.

"Ready?" I asked and when I turned around he fell backwards trying to climb over himself. I lifted it up immediately.

"It's me! It's me! Don't be afraid!"

He relaxed and grinned at it's power to transform me.

"Can I see it?" he asked.

I gave it to him and he looked at it only a second before he asked me if he could show his mate. Recognizing that grin, I said yes, but to not scare her with it. He hurried back into the woods.

Obviously he had put it on or held it up in front of his face as he entered camp, because I heard her alarm whistle followed by the thud of her feet hitting the ground at a run, when he pulled it off to show her it was only him. He brought it back to me grinning ear to ear and thanked me. He was thoroughly pleased with himself.

At the party several people eventually mentioned going to get more wood and one person thought he saw Teluke standing at the fence. This fellow was fairly intent on going after wood, even though we didn't need any. Teluke was not about to put up with a tipsy man of my people and was standing ready for him. He sent the guy a clear message that we all heard in our heads. "Don't come back here or I will kill you!"

I had done my best to insist they stay away from the woods, telling them a grouchy old man owned it and would shoot anyone trespassing. They were astounded to have all heard the message in their heads and his wife eventually talked him out of it

The next day Teluke asked me if I had fun at my party. He said they watched us the whole time and it looked like we were having fun. I told Teluke that I wished they could have joined us. He thanked me and said that it was all right. I asked him if we bothered them and he said no, that they had enjoyed watching us. He asked me what we were doing with our bodies.

"Oh, you mean dancing? Don't your people dance?" I asked curiously.

"No, you people sure do strange things with your bodies!"

I chuckled. "Yes, we enjoy our bodies. We learn to do all kinds of strange things!" I bopped around in the field dancing to the memory of last night, feeling stupid, but enjoying myself none the less. "Dancing is sort of like a mating ritual. Do you have those?" I asked humorously.

"No. Well, we have rituals..." he seemed caught up in confusion. "You mean you people have to do that before mating?"

"No, I wouldn't say that. But often when we do dance we find it sexy and then mate afterwards," I said. It had never dawned on me as to the function of dancing, but what I said was true.

The weather had begun to get poor as it does that time of year in Indiana. The nights were getting colder, often bringing with it cold rains. I worried about Teluke and his family and told them so.

One day the television had predicted a cold hard rainstorm and I wanted to take something out to them for their protection. I thought about blankets but knew they would just soak up the water. I asked them if I could bring them some plastic to cover themselves with. They didn't know what plastic was but didn't mind the idea of not getting wet.

I didn't like the idea of giving them plastic, simply because of what it was, but I didn't know what else to do. I carried out a large piece and laid it down at the front of the force field, placing a rock upon it to hold it. I explained not to leave the baby alone with it for fear of suffocation. They rejected the use of it then immediately. But I explained that it is safe if you follow the rules, which I also explained to the couple. I told them I would leave it here at the force field in case they changed their minds.

After the storm, I went out to check on them and was surprised to find the plastic had moved. It was up against the fence in the pasture. They told me to come and get it. They had tried it out but it was too noisy and they were afraid the baby would not breathe. They preferred to get wet. I found it enlightening how they held their healthy priorities. I admired them for it.

Winter came and I continued to check on them often. One night there was a blizzard and I was deeply concerned about them. But I had come to expect them to endure whatever came. In the morning schools were closed, and the earth was silenced in frozen beauty. I bundled up early and waded through the snowdrifts out to the force field. The wind stung my face and burnt my nostrils as the sun blinded me, reflecting off the brilliant snow.

"How are you guys this morning? Did you make it through the storm all right?" I asked anxiously.

He didn't answer immediately and it concerned me. "Yes, we are all right," his voice sounded miserable to me. "But the baby is awful cold. Could we use your barn?"

I couldn't have been more delighted! "Yes! That's a wonderful idea!" I exclaimed.

"Will anybody bother us in there?" Teluke asked warily.

"Not really. We don't use the barn as much in the winter. We will be in to feed twice a day and to clean stalls, but the barn won't be busy like it is in the summer. Come on, you can move in right now if you want. I will help you!"

I was always anxious to interact with them, so naturally I was disheartened when Teluke told me to go on ahead and they would follow.

I began to plow a path through the drifts with my body for them. When I turned back to see Teluke holding the baby in one arm, while helping Teleel over the fence, I slowed my pace to let them catch up some. I asked if the snow wasn't pretty cold on their bare feet, but Teluke said it wasn't too bad. I couldn't help wonder how Teleel felt, though. He spoke for them both without asking for her opinion.

From the paddock, I had to leave them at the sliding barn door to go in the side door and unlock it from the inside. I was honored that they asked me for help and I was tickled that Teleel and the babe would have to pass right by me as I held the door for them, which wasn't really necessary.

Teluke had other plans though, and made me move away from the door.

"Oh, come on!" I pleaded, "You know I'm not going to hurt you by now, don't you?"

"Move away from the door or we won't come in," he ordered flatly. He had his family with him, so things were different. It was a simple enough request so I obliged them just for the privilege of being able to help them. I felt, though, that it was a small enough request on my part in return for some of the help and sharing I had done for them. Not that much to ask, really. But I willingly put my small reward out of the way because I loved them so much.

Once inside I explained, as I shut the door, that I would have to lock them in from the inside but that they could always get out and I showed them how to work the latch.

Before I explained how, though, I heard Teleel gasp at being locked in and heard Teluke privately reassure her that he would break it down and they would get out. They both took a deep sigh when I showed them how to get out. I still hadn't earned their trust. How very disappointing!

I explained a few rules that I thought of, such as keeping the doors shut and locked and asked them if they ate hay. Teluke was amused and said not usually. I asked if they ate grain and he said yes, so I told them they could use the horses grain if they wanted, but not to use it all and to keep the lid on the barrels. I showed them the hayloft as I climbed up and I said they would be safe and left alone up there. They didn't bother with the ladder, but leaped up like it was a porch step or something. It left me feeling rather inadequate and embarrassed at having to climb.

Teluke asked if the hay pick, which was stuck in a crack in a beam, was a weapon. My stomach lurched thinking about what he could do with that if he wanted to and I told him no. I explained that it could certainly be used as one, but "Please remember that we cannot see you! We use this to help us handle heavy bales of hay!" as I demonstrated it.

"So if you see someone coming at you with this, **realize** they are not seeing you, but are just wanting the hay you are sitting on! Don't take it as a threat! It's not an attack! Just get out of the way of them and let them have the hay. They won't even know you are here!" I told them I would try to be the one to get the hay most of the time so Pop and Byron would not be a concern too often.

It began well for the most part. I tried not to bother them at all and tried hard to forget they were there. Yet, I thought I was always somewhat conscious that someone was living in the barn now. If that sounds contrary, please keep in mind that I worked on at least three levels: #1 - The conscious, which stayed pretty ignorant of it all; #2 - The subconscious or Second Attention; and #3 - Somehow a mixture of the two by storing it away in my "attic" consciousness of the First Attention.

Pop had noticed the grain going down a bit faster and it seemed at times we'd just fill the water buckets and they would be empty, but all in all it was easy to forget they were there.

I did such a good job of forgetting them that one night I had a bad fright when I went after a handy bale of hay with the hay pick. Just as I was about to lash into the bale, one of them swiftly moved out of the way at the last second, and I heard them telepathically say, "She doesn't see me!" I was just sick about it and apologized all over the place for not seeing them.

One evening Byron and I were brushing the horses and Byron was working in the cross ties where he could see into the loft. After a while, he said in an uncertain and concerned tone that there was something up in the loft moving around. I brushed it off, telling him it was probably one of the cats, but he said "Nooo," in a questioning flighty way. "This is something big! Come here and look!"

I went over beside him and saw the hay move on a bale up at the front. Hay was sticking to one of their invisible bodies and as they rose to their feet, the hay was just hanging in the air in disarray. It was rather silly looking if you knew what you were looking at, but quite unnerving if you didn't "see". The best I can describe it was that you could see where something wasn't!

"Yeah, I see what you mean! Wanna' call it a night?" I asked Byron. He agreed, so we wrapped horses' legs and went in. It was kind of creepy to see, even for me as I knew on one level what it was, but poor Byron who wasn't the bravest of souls anyway, was awfully frightened.

During the "down time" for the horses, Pop often left a radio playing in the barn to keep the horses company, which is the practice in many barns. Teluke having moved into the barn, asked me one day what that noise was and I explained to him it was music from the radio. He wanted to know what the guy singing the song was saying and I told him, "Oh, Baby, Oh, baby, I love you, I do," and explained the guy probably doesn't even know what real love is.

Teluke asked me if I could turn it off, which I did. When Pop came out to feed, he of course turned it back on and left it on, mentioning that it had been turned off, which he didn't care for. This told me that I probably should keep clear of the situation. But a few days later Pop complained that someone was screwing around with the radio. I too, had found the radio off the station and so I asked Teluke what he knew about it. He apologized and said that he didn't like the noise and was trying to turn it off by turning the knobs but couldn't find the off knob. I chuckled and told him it was a lever on the wall. I apologized for the nuisance and said I would see if I could at least get him to turn it down a bit, which seemed to alleviate the problem some.

One cold snowy day I went in and found Teleel alone. The back door into the paddock was opened just as Pop had curiously mentioned finding it a few days before. I shut it without even thinking about it. I climbed up into the loft and found her cowered against a bale covering her child with arms and legs.

"Where is Teluke?" I asked her.

She cowered even more and protected her child from exposure to me. "He went out."

I was alone with her! "Oh, oh. I just accidentally locked him out. I will open it when I leave." Thinking too, that this was a prime opportunity for us girls to chat safely.

"Can I see the baby?" I asked expectantly, as I started over towards her.

She bent over the top of her baby. "You come any closer and I will call my mate!" she said defensively.

I was shocked. I was absolutely sure, given the opportunity, Teleel was on my side about wanting to be friends. But things being as they were, I explained, "But he is locked out right now."

"That doesn't matter. He is very strong and will break your door and then kill you!" she retaliated.

I knew she was right. God, how I ached to just <u>see</u> the baby! "No, you won't have to call him," I said, as I backed off respectfully. God, how it hurt that even she did not trust me! He had poisoned our relationship with his fear. She was my childhood acquaintance. I had felt that that somehow bonded us.

"Can't you see my love for you? My honesty?" I had thought they would just know me inside, somehow. She shook her head no.

"I don't know why you guys are afraid of me anyhow! Even you could kill me anytime you wanted to! I could never hurt you and get away with it! I'm the one who should be afraid! My people are really pretty fragile. We hurt very easily! All you would have to do is take a swing at me and you could knock my head right off my shoulders! You wouldn't have to kill me to stop me, you could just break something and I would be unable to continue."

I explained this because I wanted to let them know how totally disarmed I really was and that they had every reason to not feel vulnerable.

"I would never hurt you! I wouldn't take your baby either! I love her and it would be too painful to me when she missed you! I could never do that! I have too much love and respect for you! I was hoping you would be my girl friend!" I said sadly. "I am so good with babies! I love babies! I would never hurt you in **any** way!"

Then sizing up the real situation, I went on. "But, I see you are very frightened of me. How are you guys?" I changed the subject so she would relax.

"We are sick."

"Sick?" Oh, good lord! Had I neglected my job? I was responsible for them! How do you treat a sick Sasquatch? She could die on me! Are their bodies close enough to ours that I would even know what to do? She heard my mind racing with thoughts and chuckled.

"It's okay. We will be all right. It is not that bad."

"What is it that is wrong? How are you sick?" My mind raced to the medicine cabinet for remedies. They would need it by the bottle for their weight and size. "What are you sick from?"

"The grain made us sick," she replied.

"**Oh, My God!** It **IS** my fault! I have **POISONED** you!" I was out of my mind with worry!

She laughed and said, "We will be all right! Teluke is getting medicine for us. We are just bound up and will be okay when he gets back."

"What medicine?" I was flabbergasted.

"Plants."

"Plants? You don't understand! You're not from around here! There are no plants this time of year!" I exclaimed.

"Yes, there are! There are always plants!" she affirmed.

"No, there aren't! They all die off from the cold!"

"No, they don't die. There are always plants!" she said.

"Where? How?" I didn't understand. My head swam.

"Under the ground."

"Oh! Roots!" I breathed for the first time in minutes! "Thank God!"

I realized that I wasn't needed and decided to leave before Teluke came back and found the door locked. I didn't want that!

I went back and checked on them later and they were fine. In fact, Pop had complained that somebody had shit in his barn. It was obvious to him that it was human feces. Up in the loft I had also noticed that they were emptying themselves, right up there in the loft.

"Hey, you guys! You can't be doing this up here!" I looked around at the mess. "It is going to start smelling and it will bring attention to yourselves. If Pop comes up here in the dark and steps in it, he will really get mad. Don't do it up here anymore, okay? You are welcome to use the stalls if you want. We clean them everyday."

They apologized and understood.

The next time I noticed, it had all been cleaned up. Again I found Teleel alone.

"If you come any closer, I will kill you!" she challenged me.

"Would you really kill me?" I asked in disbelief of my old friend. This hurt.

"I don't know, but I would hurt you!" she said.

"Would you feel bad about it?" I wanted to see her heart.

"I don't know. Maybe."

I looked around. "Who cleaned up the mess up here?" I asked, surprised. As long as the attention was off of them they were never defensive.

"My mate," Teleel answered.

"Well, that was awful nice of him! What did he use to pick it up with?"

"His hands," she said very simply and matter-of-factly.

"His hands?" I was mortified! "Did he have a way to clean his hands?"

She shook her head no.

"Oh, God bless him! He didn't have to do <u>that</u>! He could have used a shovel, or I could have done it myself! Bless his heart! He didn't have to do that! It wasn't that big of a deal! Tell him I am sorry about this! Tell him thank you for me, will you?"

What simplicity! How easily they cooperate with our rules. They never felt sorry for themselves and that impressed me most of all. Teluke did what he thought would be the best solution to correct the situation for the use of the barn.

# Chapter Seventeen

## A Heavy Burden

*"Light-beings across the earth*

*circle round the sphere*

*winnowing the lower forms*

*and ever drawing near..."*

POP HAD NOTICED THAT THE grain was still going down pretty fast, as well as the "skunk" that had moved into the barn. I was just keeping my mouth shut and fingers crossed that we could pull this off.

Occasionally, I would take apples out to the horses and put them in their feed boxes. One night, when no one was looking, I took a bite out of one and tossed it into the hayloft for them. The bite was to show that it wasn't poisoned and was food. I felt rather rude taking a bite out of it first, but under these circumstances I felt it was called for.

The next evening, Teluke asked me what that food was I threw up in the loft for them. He said it was good!

"An apple! Haven't you ever had them before?" This surprised me.

"No. Do you have any more?" He seemed like a child asking for a cookie. I told them that I didn't, but we would be going to the store soon and I would have them buy more. I also explained that they grow on trees. This surprised them. They didn't know food grew on trees. That surprised me! I figured they knew just about everything edible there was out there! Especially being telepathic. They should know about everything! I have no answers for this....

I realize this is incredible for a race of people dependent on nature for their survival, to not know about food from trees. Believe me, if I just wanted to create a nice novel, I would omit something so unlikely as this. But such is not the case. I feel all the facts that I have are pertinent to perceiving these being as a whole, each one being unique physically as much as mentally.

As absurd a thought as this might be, whose to say that something as fantastic as cloning adults into consciousness, programming their minds with a small history and planting them here, isn't in the agenda of the Star People? Who knows how this works... I'm merely reporting.

Also, please consider the results of total isolation. Your knowledge of food would be limited to your immediate surroundings. Realize too, that we are not speaking about a whole race, but one family. Teluke was approximately 23 years old and we do not know how old he was when he left his mother and father. If it were perhaps as young as 10 or 12 years old, his knowledge would be the sum of 10 or 12 years from where ever his parents were isolated. It appeared that he new a great deal of root foods and plants.

I make no apologies for discrepancies derived from the little data available about these beings. This family genuinely did not know. But, perhaps he just meant apples and I am making too much out of it.

He asked me if there were those trees around here and I told him I hadn't seen any, but they might look up the road sometime.

"But be careful! I don't know if there are any dogs up there," I warned.

The apples were taken freely from the horses feed boxes and I told them they might want to go slower because they might get sick from eating too many. This concerned them, but I told them it wasn't serious if they did get sick. I explained that many people risk a bellyache to eat a good apple. I told them that especially green apples are good for bellyaches.

That year seemed to be a good year for lice. I had found a nice, fallen bird's nest that was real deep and I stuck my fist down into it and when I pulled it out it was black with lice.

Pop's chickens also had to be treated for lice. The mares had gotten a few places on them that were suspicious, so we inspected and dusted them as well. The neighbor's stables had gotten a few horses in that looked lousy, so we just took precautions.

Teluke asked me what we were doing to the horses and I explained. He wanted to know what lice were and I told him it was a very tiny bug that lives on the skin and itches and makes the hair fall out. He was quiet.

"We scratch sometimes."

"Well, I know, everybody does sometimes. Do you scratch a lot? I don't believe people can get this type of lice."

"No, just sometimes we scratch. We don't want our hair to fall out. What do they look like?" He was scared; you could hear it in his voice.

I tried to explain as he sat up in the dark loft looking through Teleel's hair. I told him that it would be better if they came down and let me look, which they did.

Looking through Teluke's silky hair, for some reason I was having difficulty seeing if there were the white nits on the bases of hair shafts and told him that I really needed to check Teleel because it would be easier to spot them on her hair. I said that if one of them had any, they would all have them. I assured him I wouldn't try anything and that he could easily overpower me. So she handed the babe to Teluke and stepped over to me in the light.

Keeping to my business, I searched for a few minutes on her arm, back and head, and found nothing and assured them that I believed people lice are a different species of parasite. They took a deep breath and nodded understandingly.

As they made themselves at home in the barn, Teluke asked me one evening, "What are these little animals that come in the barn?"

Thinking he meant rodents, I suggested mice and pictured one.

"No, they are bigger. They are like dogs, but not dogs."

"Oh! You mean cats!" I ascertained and chuckled.

"Yes! They are nice little animals. They come and sit on us. They like to be touched," Teluke smiled warmly at the thought.

One afternoon my sister-in-law came into the house all excited. She claimed that she had gone out in the barn to see her cats and found one of them asleep and hovering in the air about a foot above the hay bale. This is at least how it appeared to her, as the cat snoozed in the lap of one of the Sasquatch.

My sister-in-law had seemed to have trouble raising cats, as the kittens always seemed to disappear. And, if I'm not mistaken, she came into the house one day just sick at having found one of her cat's remains after something was through eating it. I never questioned Teluke about it. It was just too horrible for me to even consider that he might eat them.

They began to ask me if I had any food, that they were hungry. I was always happy to do all I could for them! "Would you drink milk? We always have plenty of that!"

I could almost hear Teluke's gears working. "Oh? How do you always have plenty of milk? I guess we would," he answered, puzzled.

I laughed at what he must have been thinking and explained that we use cows' milk because they make so much of it.

I brought the milk and sandwiches out for them on a tray and explained how to be careful with the glasses. I told him it wasn't so important if they broke them, but that glass is hard to clean up and they could get splinters in their feet and hands or cut on a sharp piece. It is difficult to always be conscious of the fact that they are so totally ignorant of our way of life. I explained the forks in case they wanted to use them for the other food.

When I returned for the tray, they said we have strange things. They had not used the forks, though they had tried them and were careful with the glasses. They liked the milk and vegetable salad, but didn't like the bread because it stuck to their teeth. I explained that it was too bad they didn't like it, because bread helps fill us up and is made from grain. They asked if I had more food, so I went in to look for dessert. We had apple pie and there was just enough left for two nice pieces.

The Sasquatch were just as careful with the tin pan as they were with the glasses and returned it to me safely. They were in love with the pie and asked if we had any more. I was getting concerned to be making so many trips out there and was glad to be able to say it was all gone. I did end up telling Mom, when she was surprised to see all the pie eaten up, that I just had a sweet tooth attack.

I had made the mistake the first time they asked me for food, of taking them out a supply of enough food for several days. They ate it all in one sitting! It looked like I had a problem on my hands. I had to explain to them that since the family didn't know about them, that it appeared to the family that I was consuming enough food by myself for three people! They explained that they thought we had plenty of food always available!

I could see where they got that impression. I had to explain that it costs money, which I also explained, and that since it is not my money that buys it but Pop's, it was not my food. I told them that I am just free to eat what I need and that if I took three times my share I was not being considerate of the family. I personally did not have any money because I had agreed to turn over every paycheck to my husband to put towards a piece of land we were buying.

It all began to sink in that I was responsible for feeding two very large human beings, who needed to eat every day, all winter long! I began to get a real sick feeling in the pit of my stomach. I had never had to carry such important responsibility before, not even towards having a baby of my own.

I explained to them that about all I would probably be able to do was to just keep them from starving! "Please, though, tell me if you get too hungry! I can feed you some, but you aren't going to be fat by spring! I am sorry I cannot do more! If I could tell somebody and depend on them, I would be able to do more than this. But I have to keep you a secret and so my actions can't be suspicious at all. I want so badly to just have you come inside and share all that I have use of!"

Teluke was very kind about it and apologized for having abused my generosity. It broke my heart and I walked back into the house silently.

I didn't know what else to do! It caused me to fall into a depression. I would at times ask the family if I could pick out some vegetables when we went to the store, which was okay, but I couldn't ask each week. My husband gave me grief as well if I even asked for five dollars, stating that Pop pays for the food and insisted I stick to my original promise to turn over each complete check.

I hated this! I had a responsibility that I could not fulfill! Out of desperation, I secretly told Mom, when she again noticed how much food I was "eating", that I needed her help. Desperate people do desperate things.

I forgot and confided in her on the conscious level rather than the Second Attention, that I was taking care of a family who I let live in the barn. She didn't like this, so I explained further that it was the family that had a child in the woods. She didn't go for this at all, and said she didn't think Pop would either.

Boy, I was scared. I felt so sick and dizzy from fear. When she mentioned it to Pop I can only believe that he understood on the Second Attention because he thought a moment and said he found no reason to believe there was someone living in the barn and dropped it.

Zanna may have had something to do with this reaction possibly, because she was upset with me because I didn't use telepathy with Mom on the Second Attention and instead spoke verbally to her. If things were tough before, they were impossible now because Mom, who was the guardian of the kitchen, was now fully aware of my taking food out of the house and she did **not** approve!

I felt so horrible at this blunder that all I could do was abandon myself into a depression and not come out. I refused to go to the barn hardly at all and I sat up in my room glassy-eyed, cross-legged on the floor listening to Roberta Flack singing "Killing Me Softly With His Song." I was especially attracted to the line that said "he looked right through me as if I wasn't there," which reminded me of Teluke and Teleel. I played that song enough to wear the grooves out of it and never got tired of it.

Occasionally I would surface long enough to panic at my responsibility and run out to check on them. Teluke's weak voice asked for food and I was so scared for them. My God! When was the last time I fed them? I had fallen so deeply into depression and feeling sorry for myself, I had avoided life and along with it my accountable duty! I rushed them out some food for a little while, and got ill again because it was the same thing all over again. Only this time the family could not help but notice the food missing. It was worse this time! I returned to my room and my depression.

Once again I surfaced from my dark cloud and ran out to check on them. Teleel's sleepy, weak voice said her baby was hungry.

"Oh, God! No! Not the baby!" Teleel's milk was drying up because I could not keep them fed! I asked her if feeding her would bring her milk back and she said it would, so I was dutiful for as long as I dared to be. Thank God, winter was ending soon! The really bad weather was breaking.

One day I was returning home in the car with the family when we passed the Sasquatch up the road in a yard. They were looking for apples.

Apparently they had been out for a while because they were visible to the eye! Mom saw them first and pointed them out to the rest of us. I immediately telepathed to them, "Dear God, be careful! You can be seen!" Upon which they blinked out and ran for home.

Our car had already passed them when Mom spotted them. Pop stopped as soon as he could and backed up but there was nothing there now. The family agreed that they all had seen something.

When we got home, the Sasquatch were both leaping the pasture fence. Teleel didn't slow him down at all. She was equally fleet of foot. I told Teluke they had really scared me for their safety. He said they had been out a while and we both agreed it was a beautiful day to be out. He was glad to see life returning to the earth again.

The bright sun brought warmth to the frozen earth and water trickled down ice-cycles, which spattered into clear musical puddles all around the house and barn. It was one of the brilliant days when the Mother breathes her warm breath across your face and makes your eyes hurt from the sun's glare.

Teluke was in the front paddock drinking from the horse trough when I found him. He stretched his arms out wide to embrace the day and said he was glad Mother was back.

"Oh, is your Mother here?" I asked excitedly.

"No, not that Mother. Mother!" he said, portraying telepathically to me all our environment.

"She goes away and is back now," he explained.

Realizing what he meant, I explained that we call her Mother Nature or Mother Earth.

It was the first time in a long time that I had seen him up close in the daylight. I was horrified. To say he was skinny is misleading. He had lost hundreds of pounds and now was a rack of bones with skin stretched tightly across them. His huge frame seemed more than his skin could cover. His collarbones stood up, his ribs were hollow and empty and his diaphragm was nonexistent. His torso sat on top of a structure of visible hip and pelvis bones and his huge joints were quite oddly pronounced.

He looked horrible! I commented on his extreme weight loss and asked how they had survived and he said they had slept a lot. I apologized for not being able to do more for them. He didn't at all feel sorry for himself. He simply was glad things would be easier now.

He commented that they had not seen too much of me and I told him that I was sick all winter. I told him I had almost died. I said that I didn't know how else to describe it. I was dead inside my body. He asked how a person can be dead while their body is alive. I said I didn't know it was possible, but it just felt like it. He was really sorry that I had been sick and said if he had known he could have helped me.

Shortly after that they moved back out into the woods. They appreciated the fresh air. One day my in-laws and I pulled into the driveway in the car and a fire was seen in the woods at the back. When the family remarked that it was not supposed to be there, I telepathed into the woods that their fire had been spotted and could be easily seen up here. I told them to place themselves or pull a log between the fire and the house. Almost instantly the fire seemed to disappear and I was sent a telepathic "Thank you." My in-laws disregarded it then since it was 'out' now and went on into the house.

I was healed inside to know they had more food available now. They gained weight rapidly and freed this torment which ate away at my soul through the darkness of winter. The birds sang, the sun shone more, the warm southern breezes brought back the birth of the Mother Earth and inner seeds sprouted within me, bringing color to my cheeks just as with the rest of the world around me.

I left the Sasquatch to themselves as much as possible. I felt I had done enough damage. For the first time, I had begun to seriously understand the saying "some things are better left alone." I had never found a good example for that, but I was now questioning myself.

Being in the earth plane and having to exist on the conscious level for most of it, we tend to overlook the celestial aides that guide our lives. In this case, Zanna and the Star People were just as much a part of all this as I was. It was too easy to see only myself as the catalyst. It looked like "I" had bitten off more than I could chew, when in fact the Star People had carefully prepared and orchestrated the whole affair from the beginning.

What I didn't know was that the curtain was just going up. I was center stage and the spotlight was on me. I was playing my role out just as expected.

# CHAPTER EIGHTEEN

## Strike Three

"...you look around at the humus and see your leaves

scattered and decaying, permeating the air

giving life of its own...

Nothing left but silence, the dark side of day."

SUMMER JUST SORT OF TRICKLED into my life that year. I did my best to wade through the muddy parts of my life. I had put aside my cloak of despair and the sunnier days seemed to stuff it further back into some mental closet, so I was feeling more colorful and cheery each week.

I met the Sasquatch family out in the barn late one afternoon. The gorgeous evening sun was painting the shed row deep orange and cast a melancholy mood over each of us.

"We're not going to be together much longer," I told them.

"We know," they both acknowledged sadly.

"I'm sure gonna' miss you guys! I don't know what I will do without you!"

"Yes. We will miss you, too!" I'm not sure which of them did the talking, but they both agreed. Teleel held the baby closely, emanating her inner feeling of love for me and leaned her head on Teluke. I had never threatened her, even though she was still afraid of me at times.

"I wish I had a picture of you guys to remember you by," I said wistfully. Then I remembered my Swinger camera! "Hey! Would you mind if I took your picture? I have a camera! It won't hurt you at all!"

"What is a camera?" Teluke asked.

"It is a machine, a little box that takes pictures, you know, like in a book?"

"You mean you can do that too?" He looked at Teleel as if to say "Where does it all end?"

"Yeah! I will go get it!" I jumped up and started for the house. Teluke stopped me momentarily.

"We don't want you to take our picture! But I would like to see this camera."

'Oh, hell! I never get anything I ask from them!' It made me upset to have the camera in my hands and them in front of me and to be forbidden to snap just one. I only wanted it for my own use, for my memories of their beauty. I thought about taking one by surprise, but I wanted their trust more. I wanted to show them my integrity and loyalty.

When I brought it up to my face to show them how it worked, Teluke made sure they were not in front of it. He asked me if I could show him how it worked.

I handed him the camera and was, as always, euphoric to be viewing the scene from both consciousnesses. My subconscious, or Second Attention, took in both realities where it saw the complete picture. But my physical eyes saw only the physical results of their presence.

As I handed him the camera, it seemingly floated in the air and moved around as he inspected it. It is no wonder I have never taken an interest in magic acts on TV and 'Master Illusionists'. I have experienced a much more substantial "magic", the real deal!

He wanted to know if he could take a picture of me and I said "Of course!" I stood before the flash as he took the picture and we watched it manifest into a print. He asked me if I would get in trouble showing them all of our magic and I laughed and explained that to us it wasn't magic, it was science.

I told him it was free for anyone to learn whatever they wanted. I said that they could keep the photo, but they didn't want to, saying it would get ruined. This really disgusted me, and hurt. To me it said they didn't care to remember me.

Of course I knew it would get ruined, but it was only the gesture I needed from them, that was all. If they didn't want it I certainly had no reason to keep it, so I threw it aside like trash.

"Don't you want it? You will ruin it!" they said in alarm.

"No, I know what I look like. If you don't want to remember me, I don't need a picture of me, so I'll throw it away," I said, hoping to get a better response.

Teluke picked it up. "But it will be ruined if we keep it."

"Well, I know that. Just keep it until it gets ruined. Then bury it somewhere." The picture seemingly floated freely in mid air.

"Can't I take one of you to remember you by?" I asked.

They finally agreed, but told me it wouldn't come out. They said others have tried before and couldn't take pictures of their people. I told him that sometimes people catch a ghost on film so it could be possible and I should at least try.

After I took the picture, what developed was the side of the barn. They smiled sorrowfully at me.

"I guess I will just have to hold your pictures in my heart. I am afraid I will forget exactly what you look like. You are so beautiful to me! I don't ever want to forget you!"

And how easily one does forget precious moments in any case. Little shards sliver off until all that remains are crude fragments of memory. In this case I was supposed to forget it...for a time.

Byron and I had found a nice little private place in the country to swim. It was a pay lake for fishing and swimming. A privately owned business that someone had going on their land. It was public, but not well known, so it wasn't terribly crowded like some places you are forced to use for swimming.

I went out to check on them afterward, one afternoon, when we came home. The sun had gotten hot enough to really appreciate a swim, and we had been going every day.

"What do you have on your body?" Teluke questioned me.

"It's a swimsuit."

"You mean you people have different clothes?" He had seen me in little else than blue jeans and flannels, so this was new.

"Oh, yes," I laughed. "We have different clothes for different activities."

Teluke was fascinated. "What are those for?" he asked me.

"We use these for swimming around in water. Rules, you know."

"What is swimming?"

"Oh, you know, it's when you go into the water and move around to cool off. I like swimming under water best!" I never tired of explaining to them.

"You mean you people can breathe water?" he asked in surprise.

"No, we hold our breath and go under."

"How do you hold your breath? I don't understand." he was amazed at our ways.

"That is when you take a deep breath and don't let it out right away," I said.

"Don't you die?"

"No, you get another breath when you need one." It occurred to me then that they might enjoy the water as well on these hot days, so I asked them if they would like to go with us tomorrow. They reminded me that they could not stay invisible too long, but I told them it wasn't far from here and we would not have to stay long. I told them that there are not a lot of people where we go so it should be safe. They seemed to feel they might like to try it, so I told them I would let them know when we were about ready to leave.

When it was time to go the next day, I called them up to the barn and told them I needed to prepare Byron first. Teluke was startled and said I couldn't tell anybody about them, but I assured him that I would handle it "up here", pointing to my head. I explained that it was too risky for me to take the responsibility if Byron didn't know anything at all. I needed his "ignorant" cooperation.

I went over to Byron by the truck and tapped into a very secret part of his psyche and spoke inside his head. "You know how you always love things that have to do with Big Foot?" I asked, while not looking at him.

"Yes?" he responded telepathically.

"Well, I've been keeping a secret and I need your help. I have been taking care of a family of Sasquatch on the farm here and they want to go swimming with us."

Byron was momentarily upset. "What? You know I can't be part of anything like that! I'm too scared!" he replied with great anxiety.

Then I reminded him that he doesn't have to let himself know, that it is 'all right!'

Somehow I directed his attention to the fact that this conversation was taking place unknowingly to his physical body.

"This way, you can be a part of it too!" I hoped he would see the advantages of cooperating.

Realizing that he wasn't consciously aware of the conversation here, he saw that he could remain ignorant and was pleased that it worked. "Oh, yeah!" He got the connection and could do it! His telepathic response was receptive and accepting!

I waved my hairy friends over to the truck. Having "awakened" his Second Attention, Byron "saw" them. I walked by Byron and telepathically told Byron <u>not</u> to look at Teluke's feet. He looked at Teluke's three toed feet. It was just enough to weird him out.

"Look at his feet!" he yelled telepathically. His body showed signs of extreme stress. He started falling apart on me but I caught his psyche and took his attention from it. Teluke's odd feet were too much for him. By verbally speaking to Byron I switched his attention over to the conscious level where he wasn't at all aware of them.

I verbally told Byron, "Just a minute, I have to do something." He was momentarily confused as I opened the tailgate for them. In view of normal awareness there seemed to be no reason for me doing this.

"What are you doing?" he asked, verbally. Then his Second Attention saw them (because he had agreed to help), and he said "Oh, yeah!" (verbally) He turned his back to us and got on in the truck, ignoring us.

Keeping my eyes off their faces, I instructed my Sasquatch friends to sit facing the back so they could breathe easily. I told them there was no real reason they had to stay invisible once we were on the road except when we stopped, or if they saw someone out in a yard, or if a car pulled up behind us. We would be traveling the back roads where there would not be a whole lot of cars.

I noticed they were confused about knowing when to be invisible so I told them I would just tell them when. This way they could save their energy for when we were at the lake.

As we drove along, Teluke asked me what the telephone poles and silos were and I explained things along the way.

Byron's physical body was extremely nervous and fretful, and he kept wanting to look up into the rear view mirror. He wasn't sure about anything and it was causing him great physical anxiety! Telepathically I told him I would help him forget about them and then I twisted the mirror so that he could not use it at all.

Normally he would have said something, but he never questioned me. This was why I needed his acceptance of it. It was working beautifully. He telepathically thanked me for helping him this way. I had to protect Byron from a conscious acknowledgement of what was going on. His conscious ignorance was very important to his mental stability and well-being. Things were working out well, so far.

Then I happened to turn around and look out the back window. The Sasquatch's hair was flying furiously and they were enjoying the ride, but a car had pulled up behind us and the occupants were waving and flagging us, pointing to the Sasquatch in the truck bed. I yelled, "Hey, you guys! Get invisible!" and they blinked out of sight as the car pulled along side of us.

"Hey! You have bears in the back of your truck!"

I switched levels of awareness and was as totally ignorant as Byron. The car slowed down a bit to get a second look at what wasn't in our truck bed anymore. They felt foolish and whizzed on by, screaming and honking their horn.

It was pretty frightening to all of us. Teleel had wanted to bolt at the sound of the horn, but Teluke halted her, remaining calm. I had to be totally void of any knowledge of them to genuinely console Byron that those people in that car were just idiots. Byron was upset that they tried to make him conscious of the fact and we didn't say a word the rest of the way.

When we arrived at the pay lake, I had them blink back out as we pulled in. It was hot, but early, so it wasn't going to be horribly busy. Just busy enough.

There were two small ponds for fishing up on a rise and a small long pond for swimming to the side at the bottom of the rise. Small woodlots etched the borders of the ponds in several places. The swimming lake was fenced in.

When we got out, I ran around to Byron's side of the truck. He said he would go on ahead. Teluke was walking to the end of the truck to get out of the back and Teleel was going to step over the side of the truck to get out.

Instinctively, I reached to assist her and she cowered. Teluke attacked me with his snarling charge. Apparently his adrenals were still primed up from the car that had honked at us.

"Get away from my wife or I will kill you!" he snarled in his usual gorilla way that he had.

I was horrified! "I'm sorry! I was just helping her out!"

"I can take care of my wife! You get near her again and I will kill you!"

Byron physically ran to my aid and politely telepathed, "And this is <u>my</u> wife and <u>you</u> don't hurt her!"

Teluke wasn't impressed and snarled like a vicious dog and told him. "You are no match for me! I can kill you easy, too!"

A young man and woman who had pulled into the parking lot at the same time we did had headed towards us, having seen some curious creatures in the back of our truck, possibly thinking they were bears. But seeing Teluke's horrendous snarling charge, their expressions changed from curious anticipation to horror, and they detoured and made a bee-line for the gate instead.

Byron turned white and became totally ignorant of anything at all and walked away. To me it was the same o', same o', just another act of his male barbarianism. "Yeah, you can kill me. Big deal, some trophy!" were my thoughts. I am acutely aware of my inner Spirit and I am not impressed one way or another with death. I know who I am.

I told Teluke to stay close as we walked through the gate. They lagged behind about ten feet. I turned and saw this and insisted they come right up close behind me, a foot or so away, until we cleared the gate! His egotism was trying to make a smooth road lumpy here and that meant possibly trouble. I had my hands full enough with juggling Byron's ignorance and taking charge of the Sasquatchs' welfare. I didn't need his personal stubbornness!

The gate attendant was relaxed and pleasant, but then he frowned. Psychically he was aware of the Sasquatch and verbally said "Hey! We don't allow those things in here!"

I purposely switched his level of awareness by audibly speaking "accurately" for the occasion. "What things?"

He then switched back to the First Attention or regular consciousness and saw nothing.

"Oh! Ha, ha! I thought there was somebody behind you! Ha, ha. I don't know what I was thinking!"

We walked down to the water and Byron told me he was going to stay at the shallow end. I stayed with him for a while and let the Sasquatch enjoy themselves.

The interaction that day was extremely valuable to me for many reasons. I was "seeing" in a way that is other than looking. I was vividly aware of the people who could also see psychically. I could see the body of light in people around me. I knew which ones were "Godly" and who were not because the Godly ones had more light about them. There was also a difference between the intensity of those who were Godly and those who were just psychic.

One man was extremely dark inside. Zanna explained that this was what pain and hate look like. What bothered me most though was that there were children whose light did not shine. I knew which ones felt unloved and which had been abused or molested. It was extremely painful for me to see and I wanted to go nurture them, but Zanna said it wasn't my place to, and they had things to work through.

The gate attendant was fairly psychic when he was relaxed. The fellow at the concession stand could see to some degree. And there was a man on the shallow end and a woman on the other who could see quite well.

After we entered and settled ourselves, there was so much of a stir in the crowd that Teluke asked me if they could see him. I told him that most of them could not. Most of them were just reacting to the vibrational change.

I was kept extremely busy flipping back and forth from First Attention to the Second, where the Sasquatch were visible to me. When I listened to those around me, I would become just as blind and ignorant attending the First Attention as they were. When Teluke spoke to me, I was again on the Second Attention and not only could see him, but understood quite well what I was doing with them there.

I swam under water up to Teluke and told him to watch me. I dove under and came up over there. He asked me how I did that, so I explained how to hold his breath and pull himself through the water while paddling his feet. He tried it and came up sputtering. He said it hurt his nose.

I told him that it takes practice and that I blow a small amount of air through my nose to keep water out. He tried it and was off! He swam like a submarine with an incredible capacity to hold air!

While he was under water, I became aware of Teleel sitting on the beach naked. The baby patty caked and splashed in front of her. God! They were so precious!

Automatically I asked her, "Aren't you afraid of getting an infection by sitting on the ground naked?"

"What is infection?" she asked innocently.

"Illness in one place." I said telepathically, directing her attention to her genitals. She said no, her people don't get sick that way. Then she reminded me that I wasn't supposed to be talking to her.

I was horrified! It was so easy to forget! My God, I could have gotten her or myself killed! Where was Teluke? Thankfully, he was under water, I guess.

He was having a ball, swimming among the legs of other swimmers, not at all afraid to use his hands to guide himself through. People were hollering. Many people were psychically infecting the others to be psychic, also.

Conversations were such as, "What is that? Don't you see it?" "No, Marge, it's just your imagination again." "No! She's right! I see it too! Don't you?" "See George, I'm not imagining these things!"

Teluke had risen from the water. He was beautiful! He looked like a fountain! Being invisible, the water flowing from his hairy body rose up in mid air, streaming from him, falling downward into droplets of sparkles! He shook himself like a wet dog and water flew everywhere. It was remarkable how thorough a job it did. Enough water had been shook off that he was merely dusty looking in the droplets that still remained on him.

We walked onto the beach together. Having no visible body to block the sunshine from the droplets, the water drops refracted the sunshine fully like crystal jewels. Truly a marvelous visual sensation!

When we stopped, I became totally absorbed in the visual light show he was creating for me. I stood inches away from his arm staring, mesmerized in the dazzle of crystal drops.

He asked me what I was doing. I told him he was beautiful! I explained that I was looking at the water droplets on him. I also told him that now he could be seen and it wasn't very safe now. We should be going.

He said we would go in a little while. He wasn't ready just yet. He went over to Teleel and took the baby so that she could go in. Some people were walking by disgusted that they didn't have swimsuits on. Others thought those who saw anything were crazy.

After Teleel had cooled off in the water, she took the baby again. Teluke walked over onto the beach and decided to take a dump right there in front of God and everybody! I didn't pay too much attention, or maybe I just didn't want to know, until some kid walked up behind Teluke, drawing people's attention to the miraculous dung manifesting itself out of nowhere onto the sand! It wasn't invisible like Teluke was. No more so than the stream of urine I had seen that afternoon in the paddock. Yes, it does look insane! Too much of these kinds of things tend to just make one relinquish any firm attachment to things such as interpretations of sanity and realities.

"Teluke! What are you **doing**?" I asked in disbelief.

"I had to do this," he said in a half breath.

"You can't do that there! We have <u>rules</u> you know! We have a special place to do that!" I looked for a cup or something to clean it up with, but could find nothing. The trash barrel was empty because it was too early before the crowd. All I could do was kick sand over it to cover the embarrassment. Some man soon found it with his foot of course, and things went downhill from there.

Teluke and I were on the deeper end, standing, when a little boy, maybe 6 or 7 years old, waded over to Teluke wide-eyed and impressed. Teluke turned calmly and smiled kindly at the youngster, when his Grandmother yanked the child away.

I spoke up, "He won't hurt you! He loves children! Can't you see that? He is just like you and me. God made him, too!"

The woman versed adamantly (telepathically), "No, he's not! He's one of the devil's angels! Now, that's a shame because I can see you are a good person! You shouldn't hang about with those of his kind! You will see! You will go to hell for it! That's the devil's angel!"

How sad, she was able to see for herself the purity in Teluke. Not just by his light, but there was no cloudiness there within him. He was "clear". There was not a blemish of hatred or malice in him, just his fear. His heart was so pure that he appeared as transparent as his body was! He had more shine than any of the Christian psychics there! There was such darkness in the bodies of most of the people here at the beach!

An older boy waded by, as I was about to pass in front of Teluke and dive in. "What is that? Look at that!" he said pointing to the water.

I switched levels of awareness to see it as the boy saw it. To my utter amazement, there was a hole in the water where Teluke's invisible body was standing! Being on that level of consciousness, I too, was as ignorant and confused as everyone else.

I bent over to look into this curious hole. My head bumped Teluke's side and I didn't question it. I could see a perfect mold of two legs down there! I was confused. I wanted to see if I could see any fish. I went to reach into the hole and my hand slid down his side. Again I didn't question it, though I was thoroughly confused!

Just then, Teluke broke the spell by asking what I was doing. Immediately I switched attention and could see Teluke again. To my mortification I realized that I had my face inches away from his penis, which was bobbing up and down on the surface of the water.

"Oh, my God! What he must be thinking!! How must it look to him?" My thoughts flashed. I tried to explain that I was just looking into this hole; I was looking for fish; I couldn't see him... and realized by his expression that I was six foot under and digging fast!

All I wanted to do was get as far away from the nightmare of this horrible incident as quickly as I could! I dove under water and pretended it never occurred.

Byron was doing a "beached whale" imitation and was as far removed physically and mentally as possible. It looked like a perfectly delicious idea to me as well. Byron didn't have a whole lot to say and it grew hot without the water, so I meandered around a bit and went up to the arcade for a snack. Teluke followed behind.

A boy around 12 or 13 saw Teluke as he and his mother passed him. The boy said, "That's a Sasquatch!" His mother asked, "A what?" and the boy told her again Teluke's identity. Though scary, it was kind of nice for someone to guess correctly. I gave the boy a mental "star".

I got my snack and walked a few yards to open it. I had noticed the man behind me order three cokes and three cokes were set out for him. The next thing I knew, they were arguing.

The attendant was wanting the man being served to pay for three drinks because he had set three out for him. But the man being served was arguing that he would not pay for three drinks when he only got two. He showed the man that he didn't have the third drink on him and hadn't stepped away from the counter to steal it. He even went so far as to agree that he had also seen three cokes set out, but that he had not received the third and would not pay for it!

Just then Teluke walked up beside me with an invisible coke in his hand, trying to figure out how to work the straw as he saw others doing.

Realization hit me. "Where did you get that?" I shot out at him.

Very calmly he replied, "Over there. That nice man was giving them away." He was working at the straw.

"No, he wasn't giving them away! You have to pay for that with money! You stole it!" I told him. He asked me if he should take it back and I said no.

"Please! Don't do anything else without asking me first! You are getting us in trouble! Now there is a fight over there!" I wasn't trying to make Teluke feel bad, but I certainly wanted to impress upon him the consequences of his actions.

He apologized and asked how to work the straw. I told him to suck on it. He wanted to know what suck was, so I explained that it is how a baby nurses the breast.

He tried it and I encouraged him on until the coke cleared the top. He grimaced.

"It's cold!" He tried it again and grimaced again. He went over to Teleel to share it with her and brought it back over to me.

"Do you want this? I don't like it," he telepathed.

I told him yes, but that I didn't want him to hand it to me so that it would just suddenly appear in my hand as I reached out for it, because others would possibly notice.

I sidled up next to him, facing the same direction and had him put it in my hand while my arm was in a natural looking position, as if I were already holding it. When he took his hand off the cup it literally appeared in my hand, though my hand was holding it already just before he let go.

He went over to Teleel, remarking to her about the cold drinks we use. She seemed to ponder these things as well.

People all around now had become psychically infected by the two main seers who couldn't keep their mouths shut. Teluke's partial visibility from the water droplets didn't help matters either! The man at the shallow end was standing there with his hand to his brow, peering at Teluke, pointing him out to anybody that cared to see him. The whole beach was upset. It was curious to be able to see what was taking place.

There was a definite something about the two main seers that told me they could see. There was just a <u>knowing</u> this. I could distinctly tell which others were on the verge of seeing at any moment from the psychic "infection", and I could tell who could not see at all. It was like a virus that spread like poison ivy! The vibrations were at a saturation point where it was fueling the fire. Many could 'see' the strong vibration, which in turn encouraged even more people to see!

The man on the beach was really upset. "What the hell is that? It looks like a god damn bear!" Others were agreeing with him and as a whole, the place was near panic.

Teluke was minding his own little business and didn't seem concerned about the conversations going on about him. This is psychic etiquette. As with telepathy, one is not supposed to listen in on others' thoughts unless it is sent out to you, so he had shut it off pretty much.

The big mouth who was most upset went over to the concession stand and told the fellow there that there was a bear on the beach. When he pointed Teluke out to him, the concession man then "saw" him and got on the loud speaker. "Mr. Miller, would you please come down here immediately... and bring your gun!"

I was horrified! I telepathed to Teluke that they were getting a gun and to get out of here! He ran to Teleel and grabbed her up by the arm. She whistled her alarm "bird whistle" and they were out the gate in a flash. I telepathed for them to run to the truck and I would follow shortly, but they headed for the woods at the back and said that they would call for the star ship.

People began screaming and running before the speakers stopped reverberating from the announcement. I stayed put, thinking that now that the Sasquatch were removed, things would die down soon, and we could leave peacefully. I wandered over to the concession stand as the manager came with some kind of rifle or shotgun, loading it as he ran.

The snack attendant told him that it was all right now, that two bears had run out of here to the woods out back. The manager found it incredible, but he could tell by the crowd's reaction and how empty the place was now, that something really was going on! He ran up the hill to go look for himself.

"Oh, my God!" I thought. I was near panic myself, now! It wasn't settling down at all! I ran after the man with the gun. Byron appeared comatose on the beach.

I pleaded with the man to just let them go, but he ignored me. When I got up the hill to the fishing lakes, I hesitated as to what to do from here. I touched in with Zanna, while my physical ears were hearing the men around me talking excitedly about hunting the bears.

She spoke to me, "This is it, child. Teluke has to learn whether this world is good or bad."

"Will he really get killed?" I couldn't believe it wasn't a night mare and things wouldn't be all right when I woke up!

"Somebody has to die. Will it be you or one of them?" she asked me solemnly.

"One of them? You mean any of them could get shot? Even the baby?"

"Someone has to die," she repeated most calmly yet assuredly.

"But I don't want to die!" I told her.

Zanna simply acknowledged it. "Then one of them will."

Realizing it had to be a snap decision, the spell was broken when I heard Teleel's soft voice exclaim, "He's going to shoot!"

"Noooo! Not the baby! She's my baby, too!" I won't let them shoot you! I'll catch the bullet for you! I will put myself between you and the gun!" I yelled telepathically as I ran to them.

I wanted to blanket them with my body! It was a waking nightmare! I was caught between my overpowering love for my friends and the dread of catching the very real bullet myself! My heart was pounding as though it would leap out of my chest. Oh that it would, to spare me this nightmare! The blood rushing to my head made things blurry and all the more confusing to me!

The man yelled at me as I ran past his gun. "Lady, get out of there! There is a bear in there!" He was taking aim.

Barefoot, I crashed my way into the woods, injuring my feet on sticks and forest debris, but not feeling a thing.

Teluke was holding Teleel in his arms who had the baby sandwiched between them. Her little eyes were wide and frightened, too. They were terrified.

"Where's the ship?" they demanded.

"I won't let them shoot you! He won't shoot, maybe, if I am in the way! He knows he will get in serious trouble for shooting me. Let me go with you!" I pleaded.

"No, we can't go until you leave! The ship is here! Go, so we can leave!"

"Lady! Get out of the way! I have the gun cocked! I'm going to shoot!" came his brassy voice. I looked out of the trees at the raised gun pointing at me. I was sick at heart. I didn't want to be shot by some imbecile who needed to feel superior by killing innocents.

A teenager had stepped into the woods from the side and said kindly, "Lady, you better get out of here. There is a bear in here!"

I switched levels of awareness to his perception.

"A bear?" I was confused, yet I knew. My Second Attention joined in and took control. "No! Can't you see they are people? They are my friends!"

Having spoken to him from the Second Attention, he was then opened to see also.

"Oh! Yeah! I guess they are!" he said, surprised that he had not noticed.

The ship was hovering over the woods, vibrating a low hum like a refrigerator.

"Please! Take me with you!" I begged them again.

"No, please go!" They began to disappear into the ship's light beam and enter the ship.

Broken hearted, I called the boy to come out with me so they could leave. The manager lowered his gun and cussed me out. He had been wanting to kill a bear for a long time and had missed his shot on a recent hunting trip, and I had caused him to miss this one! He was furious with me. His aura flashed red, then darkened like an eclipse from his loathing of me.

I walked back up to the lakes. The huge ship hummed audibly, creating what felt like a static charge in the air from its corona. There was a smell like hot electrical wires. The ship was huge and surpassed the size of the woods. It was the usual domed shaped saucer that I am so accustomed to.

People were yelling, "Oh, My God! It's a flying saucer! Those were creatures from outer space!" Other folks could not see the ship at all. Everyone was in a state of confusion, as well as myself, who was now completely ignorant of everything.

I went to Byron, who met me inside the swimming lake fence. "Are you ready to go, yet?" he asked me, quite undaunted by the commotion. I got my towel and we headed for the gate. The attendant scowled at me and verbally said, "Don't you ever bring those things back here!" I started to comment on his bigotry, but didn't. We just left.

Byron was physically annoyed at the place. "That was the weirdest thing! I wonder why they got the gun?" he said, placidly.

From the truck I watched as the huge ship glided effortlessly across the road over us. I telepathed to them, "Are you in there?"

"Yes, we are here," came their soft reply.

"Are you going to leave? Where will you go now?" I had to assume it was all over for me. I had really blown it this time!

"We will go to your woods," came their reply.

I was greatly relieved. But how was this going to affect our relationship? I had allowed them to come into jeopardy! I felt an overwhelming weight because I had brought them here thinking it was safe and they almost got shot! I had even put the baby in jeopardy!

# CHAPTER NINETEEN

## Never Say Never

"...and the trees shook off their dew

and it rained upon me all and complete consciousness,

and I was no longer..."

WHEN WE GOT HOME, I ran to the pasture gate. "Are you back there?"

"Yes, we are here," they answered from the woods. There seemed to be no anger in their reply.

"I am so sorry about that situation! I guess it wasn't such a good idea after all!"

"That's ok. It felt good anyway," they said light heartedly.

Jeez! I was hurting inside with remorse for my carelessness. I couldn't at all accept his appeasing attitude about this. What had happened was unforgivable!

I avoided the woods and pasture for the next few days. Any trips outside the house were fleeting so I would not be noticed, and if he saw me and headed up to the barn, I went back inside. I didn't want to remind them I was even here.

Teluke must have been watching for me because he eventually caught me outside. He asked me if I would meet him in the pasture.

'Oh, God! Here it comes!' Blood rushed to my head, my ears rang, I broke out in a cold sweat. I dreaded how he was going to lash into me for this one!

I walked out into the field. He met me more than halfway. I kept my face to the ground. I was not about to provoke him by looking at him!

"You were going to let yourself get killed the other day. Why would you do that?" His voice was full of disbelief and great compassion, and startled me into glancing up at his face momentarily. He had a curious expression as he looked down at me as if I were a small child. I quickly averted my eyes back to the ground.

"God! I wouldn't let anything happen to you if there were a way to stop it. I love you so much! Don't you know that! It is a blessing to be in this world and it means so much to you! I want you to be blessed with your life!" I said, sobbing.

I am not especially a crybaby, but my love for them was so intense and so loaded with responsibility that his compassion for me caused a big rock to form in my throat and the more I tried to swallow it down, the more it scratched and formed tears. My chest heaved as I suppressed sobs, disdainfully rubbing away tears before they fell.

"But you shouldn't do that!" It sounded more like a question. "You have as much right to be here as anyone else!"

That thought was completely foreign to me. I never considered my rights as a rule. Whenever I had, someone was always there to override them. "I do?" I asked. My life was never my own, it has always been at least Gods first.

He laughed, "Well, yes! You were put here, too! You don't have to do that for anyone!"

All my life it had seemed my place to have to beg others just for the right to exist. Just for space to **be.** No matter how hard I tried to please others or be agreeable, my rights were never considered. It was never good enough and I was forced to give up my portion. It was completely foreign to hear that I had a right to my space. I never had any rights before. Where did this enter in?

I told him I would think about it and thanked him.

"Aren't you mad at me?" I had to ask.

"Mad? No! It wasn't your fault," he said, trying to reassure me.

I could not accept this. "Yes, it was! I should have never taken you there! You could have been shot because of me!" As far as I knew at the time, I was responsible for other people's actions, which of course is not true!

I avoided them then. I was totally ashamed that it had ever happened. I was completely careless to have taken them there at all.

It seemed I may have been right about one point after all, I figured. Some things <u>are</u> better left alone. I didn't yet understand that sometimes fate plays a hand in our lives and that there are many times when no one is at fault.

Teluke couldn't have punished me more than by forgiving me. I would have been better off if he had knocked me across the field, or so I felt. I took the whole weight for jeopardizing them, the baby most of all!

My life had become miserable. I fell into another depression, feeling sorry for myself. I would not acknowledge Teluke's forgiveness. It was as if he was still that grouchy old man who always snarled and attacked me when I looked at him. Only the angry part of Teluke stood out in my mind. It was all I would allow. It justified my hurting myself in his stead.

I didn't go outside much at all. When I did begin to venture out more often, I was relieved that they were not around. They began coming up less frequently and when they would try to talk to me, I merely answered their questions and went on with my business. Facing my death caused me to focus strongly on his last attack and the realization that I had been threatened by death all along in our relationship.

One day I snuck out to the barn for a quick bareback ride. The barn was dark and cool and I felt safe. Teluke popped around the corner and playfully ran up to the shed row at me to surprise me. "Hi!"

I yelled and fell backwards into the bridles, upon which he yelled and fell back from me. When he saw I had just been scared he asked, "What's wrong?"

"Oh, it's you. I thought you were going to kill me!" my adrenals pumping made me feel angry.

"Kill you? Why?" he looked so innocent and boyish, smiling.

"Well, you're always threatening to. This time I though I had had it!"

He frowned and looked at the floor. Not wanting to start an argument, I changed to a lighter subject.

"I haven't seen you guys around much lately."

"You haven't been out here much!" he retorted.

I was still feeling excess adrenaline and his words angered me.

"You mean you were coming up here because of me? I had decided to confront the issue and make him admit something, give something in return!

"Well, of course!" Teluke answered in surprise.

"But I didn't think you liked me!" I was hurting and wanted him to elaborate on this.

"Well, of course we like you!" He didn't seem to understand.

On the conscious level, I really was surprised to find this out. For a good while now, I had received only the nasty side of his actions towards me. I wanted his friendship. I needed his love! I was hurting. I was angry and I didn't know who at!

"Well, your people sure have a funny way of showing it! I thought you were coming up just because the Star People said you had to! That's not how my people show they like someone. You are always talking about how much better your people are than mine, but I don't see how you are much different than the bad ones of my people! You aren't nice to me at all! You haven't become a friend.

"You are still afraid of me! Watch!" I gently placed my hand on his chest and he flinched away predictably.

"See? Friends aren't afraid of each other. I'm not even allowed to touch you! I'm not allowed in your camp, I'm not included in games of yours, and you are always snarling and attacking me and threatening to kill me! Well, I figured it's just a matter of time before you do kill me! And all I've ever done to you was love you!" My eyes were filled with tears and that sharp rock had gotten back in my throat somehow. It wouldn't swallow!

"Well, no thank you! I don't associate with people in my world like you. I shouldn't hang around with you either, just because you're otherworldly! I can find better friends in my own world and I don't have to worry about being killed every time I turn around or make a mistake." My eyes spilled over from pain.

I hadn't realized I was keeping all of this in. It had truly hurt me all year that I had not fully been accepted as a real friend. Small acts of endearment, such as placing my hand on his back while I explain something was immediately curtailed. Things like offering Teleel a helping hand out of the truck brought on reproach. I hadn't even gained enough of their trust to look at the baby from 10 feet away! It all hurt so much and it had surfaced. I swallowed that stupid rock in my throat and turned and went out of the barn into the bright sunshine.

Teluke was so shocked that he never said a word, but stood there wide-eyed, listening.

When I got outside the barn I heard him sobbing telepathically, as he stood in the barn. "Consider yourself touched by words!" I retorted to his pain.

I hesitated then started across the yard. He entered the pasture and let out a scream into the other dimension that made the dogs jump and the birds in the trees fly out. I feared the whole neighborhood would hear and I tried to hush him.

He yelled back, "I don't care! Let them hear!" His scream reverberated throughout the nearby farm houses. Then he broke down and bawled whole-heartedly. Teleel ran out to him instantly, asking what's wrong.

"She said we were not her friends!" he began to explain.

"Be sure to tell her the whole thing! Tell her why!" I called out to him. I didn't need her to be resentful as well.

Actually, I was in somewhat of a shock myself. I had not at all expected this kind of reaction! I didn't think it would matter one way or another to him. My heart hurt for him and I started out there to him.

"I'm sorry, I didn't mean to hurt you!" I really wanted his friendship, but he stopped me.

"No! Are you saying you didn't mean what you said? Were you lying?" He screamed at me like an angry child.

I couldn't believe this, still playing games. "No, I meant every thing I said. But I said, you were not my friend! I am still your friend, as I have been all along. I just won't be around much. But I will still be here if you need me!"

I had been true in my words. I didn't care to continue being treated this way any longer. I had worked hard for a whole year to earn his trust and to make a real friendship out of this.

True, I had not really given them a fair chance to improve the relationship since the swim, but I felt I knew what I could expect from them. Besides, I wasn't really sure whether he was crying from the pain of losing a friend, or whether it was from having failed to do as he was told by the Star People, which was whatever I told him to do, and that was to be my friend.

About two weeks had passed before I thought I would check to see how he was.

"How is he doing?" I asked openly into the woods.

Teleel answered, "He hasn't said anything since that day." Her voice was concerned. "I am worried about him. He won't eat."

"He hasn't? It has been a good while now!" I was astonished. Teleel acknowledged it.

"Why is he reacting this way?"

"He loves you!" she said warmly.

I was deeply touched. I loved Teleel so much and though she and I were kept apart, we understood each other like true sisters. There was no need ever to be jealous. What we communed with was very ancient.

"But I didn't think I really mattered one way or another to him! He has continued to be so nasty at times, and all I am guilty of is loving you! I really didn't think he liked me! I thought he was just doing what he had to do! Is there anything I can do to help him? I really didn't mean to hurt him!"

Teleel didn't know what I could do. I sat quietly in the alfalfa. I wanted to help him get over this.

"Tell him that I am sorry I hurt him and that I didn't mean to. Tell him I love him," I told her.

She smiled in acknowledgement and I left the field. He would have to overcome this himself. I wasn't going to grovel for forgiveness for my words. If it was in him, he would forgive.

I went back out in another week and Teleel said he was starting to eat and say a few words.

Byron and I were divorcing. The shock of my otherworldly friends had taken its toll on our relationship. Teluke was not the first Sasquatch he had helped me assist and he never really could forgive me for his introduction to the Star People. It all had laid dormant in his subconscious, causing a psychological rejection of me.

The course of my life had changed. I decided to move out. When things wound up to the point of leaving, Zanna was talking while I packed my things.

"Don't you want to say goodby?" she asked me.

"No! He hasn't made any attempt to forgive me." I didn't even want to think about it. It hurt too deeply. My eyes passed over a tiny teddy bear in the closet that I had not been able to give a friend for her baby shower.

"What about the baby?" she prompted me.

I burst out bawling. "Yes! God damn it! The baby still loves me!" I picked it up and examined it for anything that might cause her harm. Defiantly, I pulled the eyes out even though they were attached well. I would not take any chance of her hurting herself by loose eyes, possibly swallowing one.

I tucked it under my belt and went out into the pasture to my power spot and sat down. "I came to say goodbye," I announced.

Teluke came to the fence without hesitation.

"I brought the baby a gift."

"Goodbye? Where are you going?" his response was that of surprise.

"I am moving away. Byron and I are getting a divorce," I said.

"What is divorce?"

"We are going our separate ways, going our own ways."

"I am sorry that your mate was not good to you," he said apologetically.

"Oh, it's not that. He was good to me. He just doesn't love me anymore. I guess the Star People and you guys were a bit much for him," I replied.

"I am sorry for that. We will be leaving soon also," he said. I asked when they were leaving.

"Before it snows again, we hope." His voice sounded tired.

I had a lot to say. "I brought the baby a gift. At least <u>she</u> still loves me!" I paused while he thanked me. "I am really broken hearted. I have loved you so much! I have given you food, helped you use the barn, protected you and your family with my life, and worried constantly about you and your family. Yet you still snarl and attack me. You won't let me come close to the fence or into your camp. I can't touch you!" Then I added, "You won't even let me see you! Well, all I've ever done was love you all! I am here to say goodbye now. I would at least think that all I have done for you deserves a hug goodbye!" I felt him soften at the thought.

"Haven't I proven myself to be a friend?" I was crying. This whole deal had been so painful all the way around. It was just instinctive for me to love anything that was that pure inside.

"Yes, you have." His voice was genuine and serious.

"Then let me have a hug," I asked of him. He said no.

"I can make you give me a hug!" I reminded him.

"You said you would not make me do anything I did not want to. Are you saying you lied?" he questioned me.

I was disgusted. "No. I wouldn't receive any good from it, if you didn't want to give it. But haven't I proven to you I'm a friend? That deserves something! Can I at least see you?"

"But I thought you could see us! You look right at us!" He spoke in surprise.

"No, I only see you with my third eye," I said.

"You mean you people have three eyes?" he exclaimed in awe.

"No, we only have two. But we have a way of seeing with our foreheads." I pointed to mine. "But just once, I would like to see you with my eyes!" I pointed to them as well.

He was silent for a moment. I could feel strong emotions coming from him.

"Well...come closer to the fence and I will let you see me."

I rose up and was excited when he only stopped me about ten feet from the fence. He began to materialize visibly to me for the first time! I was struck with awe!

"Oh, Dear God!" I said, just before my legs buckled under me. The shock of what I was seeing dropped me to the ground. He blinked right back out immediately and was no longer visible to my eyes.

"Please! Come back! I didn't see you well!" I pleaded as I struggled to my feet. "I didn't expect you to be white and have blue eyes! You are as beautiful as I knew you would be! Oh, my God! **Please** come back!" I was bawling without reservation. I feared he was being his ornery self again and I was on the verge of collapse about it!

He materialized again. "I thought I had frightened you! Most of your people are afraid of us!"

**"Oh, My Dear Lord God! No! You are so beautiful! I am so blessed! I am so Blessed!"** I was beside myself! On every level of my soul I was in shock. The Native Americans have long revered any white rarity to be extremely sacred. I didn't know this on any conscious or physical level at that time, but the Old Native Woman in me took its importance in full!

As a human child, I knew the odds of facing a Sasquatch, let alone a white one! I never knew there were such things. Yet there I stood, completely conscious before a fully materialized rarity by several measures.

My love was reverberating louder in vibration than I had ever felt it. He told me of whiteness, that it meant he was a Shaman. I had never heard the word before, so he clarified it by saying he was a medicine man, a doctor. That I understood! I literally bawled.

"Oh, my God! I love you so much! Won't you let me have a hug or at least touch you?" I begged. He was smiling and deeply touched. He paused a moment and said compassionately, "Well, we better keep the fence between us...but I will give you my hand," as he held it out to me.

I ran over to him, causing him a moment of uncertainty. I saw that he had wanted to flee, but he had held himself in place.

I grabbed up his huge squat hand with both of my tiny ones and kissed it without even thinking. He smiled at me. I became absorbed into what I was actually doing. I had to verify this as a physical reality. I ran my fingers in the hair on his forearm as I had so long yearned to do! Without thinking, I got carried away and fluffed the long hair back and forth on up his arm causing him to flinch away at my forwardness.

"Oh, my dear Lord!" I bawled at his absolute density. "I don't know what to do with myself! Do you know how special this makes me?" I asked, knowing there had never been anything outstanding about me before.

He shook his head "no".

"I have to be the only person in the whole world right now who is shaking hands with a white Sasquatch!"

He chuckled and agreed.

I realize now that my Second Attention had always seen the contrast between Teleel's dark color and Teluke's white hair. It was most evident when I inspected them for lice. That was why I had to inspect Teleel instead. She was a deep black/brown like a black bear that is sunburned. He was quite the opposite! I had done a completely thorough job of keeping my First Attention out of it! It was a total shock!

"God! How much I love you!" The floodgates opened and my eyes spilled freely down my face. For the first time, I was truly allowed to look Teluke in the eye! He was crying also! His compassionate blue eyes were filled with tears and they were spilling over with mine!

He said to me in return, "I know! I can feel it! You feel good to me! I love you too!" I knew beyond all doubt that he was speaking from the heart.

I went on, trying to form words between sobs. "We should be saying hello, not goodbye! This is what I have been trying to give you all of this time! This is how it is supposed to be when people meet! Not when they say goodbye! I don't want to be doing it this way! I want this to be hello!"

My love was so overwhelming, I could see it was infecting him! His smile had blown wide open. He was unafraid of me now, as he leaned into our clasped hands. He totally accepted me right then.

We were just inches away from each other's faces. I felt his breath. I saw his individual hairs and pores on his skin. His eyes spilled as freely as mine as he listened to me. He was totally unashamed of the emotions he was feeling.

I couldn't get enough! I asked him for a hug, but he just gave me a smile that acknowledged that he understood. He opened up to me as a true friend.

"Can I come live with you?" I asked.

"Well, my people have been known to take one of your people in as family before. You would have to give up smoking though," he warned me.

"That's okay, I have been wanting to anyway..." I put my head down in shame though, "but I can't. My body is addicted to it. The plant is inside me," I explained.

"Well, I could take care of that!" he said as if it were no problem.

"You could? Wow! I will consider it then!" I said. My thoughts turned to how my living with them back there would draw attention to them.

"We sure had fun sneaking up to the barn to watch you!" he smiled.

"Did you sneak up to the barn? Why?" I asked. I was working fully on the conscious level now. My First Attention was being allowed to integrate information that had previously been withheld.

"We would see the lights on in the barn and hear you having fun with your friends and wanted to see what was going on. At first we thought it was a fire and we didn't want anyone to be hurt. But then we heard you laughing," he was smiling at the memories.

"Was that you that put your hand on my shoulder that night?" I scolded.

He was definitely pleased with himself! His eyes sparkled as he grinned and said, "yes".

"That wasn't very nice of you! Do you know you made me almost shit in my pants?" I chided him.

He paused to think about the words and then realized the humor in what I had said. He started to laugh and then halted as he thought some more before really catching on to it and broke out laughing with abandonment!

The sound of his laughter was the most haunting and spine-chilling laugh I have ever heard. It frightened me so that I had to do a reality check and ask him if he was laughing. For an instant, it sounded so demonic that I was concerned he was laughing at me and not with me. But the sparkle in his eyes when he assured me he was, calmed my fears.

From what I have learned from others since then, this is one of their doctrine of signatures, a laugh that belies their pure soul and gentle nature.

"Do you understand what I just said?" I asked him.

"Yes, I learned a lot of your words listening to you in the barn," he explained.

I went on. "I thought I had seen you out in the paddock laughing at me in your 'sporty' self!" I said.

He nodded his head that I had seen correctly. I could see indeed that he had enjoyed himself! I told him that I found it hilarious to see their little red eyes blinking in the field. I had enjoyed them as much!

He said, "You really scared me when you fell off your horse that day!"

"Yeah! I could have been killed! It really scared me, too!"

He continued on, "I was coming up to help you when I saw that you were all right."

"You were going to help me? What would you have done?" I asked him.

"Carried you back to the woods and treated you. I'm a doctor."

"You would do that for me?" I asked. I was overwhelmed. It had never occurred to me that he liked me enough to take care of me. Since I was working on the First Attention, the conscious level with him for the first time, all the other interactions were very dreamlike, much like encounters with the Star People are. Underneath, though, I sensed that we had some kind of a friendship, but it was clearer that he was tenaciously skeptical of my people and me.

"You really surprised me how strong you were the first day we met," he said.

"I did?" I couldn't see how that could be.

"Yes! You really gave me a workout!" He seemed proud of me.

I said to him, "The reason I quit was because I got sick to my stomach and then forgot what I was trying to do."

He laughed at this. "You are really strong! I am a strong man and you gave me a work out! You really surprised me how strong you are!"

I was dazed by his words. 'How about that! He says I am a good match!' My thoughts were to myself, but I discussed it with him.

"All I could think of was that you were some kind of tree spirit. I have never been kicked out of a woods before. Tree spirits always love me! They used to come seeking me out at dark time when I was little!" I said.

He seemed disappointed. "We are not trees!" he said offended that I would not know this.

"Oh, I know you are not trees! But, at the time all I could figure was that you were something <u>like</u> tree spirits!" I reassured him.

"What is spirit? You use that word a lot," he asked me.

"Spirit is the part of the tree that is real and comes out of the body at night!' I said. He understood me then, as he raised his face and eyebrows.

I went on, "Then, I thought you were the devil, himself! I was fighting for my soul!"

"What is devil?" he asked me.

"The devil is the 'bad' part of the whole. The opposite of good, God. He is the one who hates and kills." I didn't know for sure where I was going with this. So much I was uncertain of, but I wanted to explain what others had caused me to understand about God vs. the devil.

When I spoke of spirit and God and reincarnation, he always seemed pleased. "You really know a lot," he told me.

He and I were relating very well intellectually. He pointed out a contrast of myself to others of the dominant society. I saw what he meant. Most people don't care to risk accepting truth about reality. Most are afraid to challenge themselves to seek further, underneath, the foundations of what is called "reality" or accept that they are infinite beings that are body identified, which is a contradiction that creates our fear, THE JUDGE.

I told him that it took me a day or two to realize they were Sasquatch. Even as a child, when I first met Teleel on the Star ship, it never dawned on me that Teleel was one. They were just people.

Their reality is just hidden in such a different realm than one would expect, that when it is encountered, it doesn't fully register what it is. One is looking straight ahead but it slips up beside you while you are walking, searching, and continuing to look for this other, this non-ordinary reality. Like looking through a reflection in a store window. You just are not aware.

"How did you beat me?" he asked.

"Beat you? I don't understand," I answered.

"Yes, in the battle!" he explained.

I laughed. "Oh! Well, the hardest part was getting you out to face me! I played a trick on you. I pulled the oldest trick my people have. It is so old that it doesn't even work any more."

"What is that?" he asked.

"I spoke bad about your Mother! By the way, I am truly sorry for what I said about her. I didn't mean it! I used it only to get you mad so you would fight me! My people know that if you want to get someone mad at you, the quickest way is to speak badly about their mother, because everybody loves their mother.

It doesn't work any more with us, because it has been used so much that if we hear it, we know someone is trying to provoke us and so we ignore it. But I knew you didn't know this, so I used it. It worked real good, too!" I laughed. "But I truly am sorry for dishonoring your Mother with it. If I met her, I would love and honor her as I do you! I am sure she is sacred and holy!"

"Thank you for saying that. That makes me feel good. But if you didn't mean it, why did you say it? You told me you don't lie!" Teluke was pretty serious. He had me there.

I explained about white lies and he started to walk away from me. "Well, I had to get you out to face me! You didn't mind it when I lied to protect you about the garden incident! It was the only thing I could think of!" I was concerned that this was about to mar what we were sharing, but we stepped passed it.

As we talked together, sharing as real friends for the first time, we squeezed hands like dear old friends. Emotions were flowing like the life force flows through the stem of a growing flower.

"God! I can't say enough how beautiful you are to me! Please can I touch that beautiful face of yours? Please? I won't hurt you!" I pleaded. It was unreal to me that he should still have any fear of me left. He shook his head no with a warm expression on his face.

"I don't understand why you are afraid of my hands! Hands are for loving! Not hurting! Look at them!" I held them out to him.

"I have nothing in them to hurt you with. They have no teeth on them. My teeth are up here!" I pointed to my mouth. "My hands are small, they are soft and they don't do anything I don't want them to! I love you! I am not gonna' hurt you with them. They are just like your hands only smaller! Please, let me touch your face!"

An idea came to me. "Here! Let me put them up there and you can put your face into them so you will be touching me!" I slowly lifted my hands up and held them four to six inches out from his face. He cautiously leaned into them. I began to mesmerize in whisper, to calm him.

"Oh, so beautiful, so soft. God, you are so beautiful to me, so soft. I won't hurt you. I won't hurt you. I love you." I soothed with my voice as well as my hands. I let my hands speak for me also, as I gently caressed his face and cheek hair. I slowly touched the hairless places of his beautiful rugged face and ran my fingers lightly over his mouth and nose and eyes. He didn't seem to mind.

"There, now how did that feel?" I asked when I was through.

"Nice," he said.

"You can touch my face if you want," I extended the courtesy.

He quickly touched my face with deft hands, poking me in the eye and was done. He didn't like to touch.

Since this was the first time I had been with him when he was fully in this dimension, physically manifested before me, I was unprepared for the aromatic difference that accompanied his presence. I was becoming overwhelmed by a stench that no longer resembled a skunk, but smelled more like I had stuck my head inside a horribly yucky garbage can!

"What's that smell?" I asked. My eyes were watering for a different reason now.

"It's me. Does it bother you?" I couldn't tell what attitude he spoke with. I was not about to offend him. I had to be as delicate as possible.

"Well, no. I just didn't know what it was," I said truthfully. I was embarrassed. The way it wafted around, it occurred to me that he had possibly farted, as he had been known to do so freely. But I then remembered that Sasquatch were supposed to smell bad in some way. I realized then that it would take some getting used to if I chose to ever live with him and his people.

It appears that they have a skunk musk that is natural to their body, and when emotions are strong, be it anger, love, fear, or joy, it creates this other smell, comparable to garbage, septic or carrion, as I have also found.

He found more to talk about. "I will tell my people what you have taught me about dogs," he seemed proud.

"You will? Well, please be careful! Tell them to weigh each situation by itself! There may be a time when running is the best choice. I would feel terrible if someone stood their ground and got hurt!"

He assured me he understood. As he gazed at me, he seemed to be fixed on a focal point just above my head.

"You know," he began, "you used to be a great Medicine Woman! Well, you still are, but you will be again. You are a keeper of the Peace shield! One day you will remember!"

"I did? I am? What kind of shield?" I asked. I didn't know much of what he spoke of, but it sounded delicious to me. I had always naturally leaned towards Native American ways, and had a deep reverence for them, but anything I did that was Native was purely instinctive and not educated into me, so to speak. I had read absolutely nothing at that time about the Native cultures.

He went on. "It will come back to you later."

"How do you know these things?" I asked.

"I can see it up there!" he said pointing with his chin to above my head.

I didn't know what he was seeing, but I assumed it was something he was reading in my aura.

Teluke said he had better go now. He said his wife had called him twice already and he didn't want her to get jealous.

"Can she hear us?" I was delighted she had not been cut off from me as I apparently was to her.

"Yes. She is not supposed to be listening, but she is," he said, smiling warmly.

"But there is nothing for her to be jealous about! I love her too! Had you allowed she and I to touch at the heart also, then she and I would be as close as you and I and there would be no jealousy! Now it is lop-sided to where she can be! I have wanted to love her too!" This exasperated me. If he had not kept us apart she and I would have grown close also, and this would not have been allowed to happen!

"May I say good-bye to her?" I asked.

"Well, since you asked first, I will see if she wants to."

I was appalled that he would stick this stupid ego "power" thing into our last moments together. I could order him to any time and he had to obey me! But I left him his dignity and allowed him to believe he had "the power".

He turned his head to the side and quietly asked her if she wanted to say good-bye. I had expected to just telepath into the woods and speak a moment, but to my great joy she mashed the undergrowth down with her heavy strides and came forward to stand beside Teluke, fully manifested into this plane of existence!

She had the child on her hip and they were both beautiful! I had kept my eyes off of them and not noticed the child any more than necessary so it was shock to see how big the child had grown!

"Oh, my Dear Lord! You brought the baby out! Look how big she is!" I paused a moment to think. "Well, I guess it has been a year!" I reminded myself out loud. But the child was the size of a five year old in our race of people. I was again overwhelmed with emotion.

"Oh, God, look at her! She is beautiful!" The child was smiling and active in Teleel's arms. When she noticed me, she beamed a big smile and turned to her mother, saying "Look Mother!" pointing at me.

I was bawling again and had my hands to my mouth. I was so overcome by the reality of what was going on in my life at that moment, I truly didn't know how to handle it! It was overkill. I was so full of emotion, I just didn't have any more room to express it. Seeing the three of them standing fully visible, a black Sasquatch, a white one and the most beautiful hairy child I had ever seen. Where do I put this?

"I am so happy! God I love you! Just look at the three of you! You are so absolutely gorgeous! Oh, God! I don't know what to do with myself! I have never been this happy before! I have never felt this way! I AM SO FULL!" I bawled and danced in place, my feet racing with my heart. I just couldn't contain anymore!

They were beaming wide grins at my emotion which I am sure they too, felt.

"Can I hold her?" It was just so natural to ask, that it didn't occur to me that they might turn me down. To my great delight Teleel started to lift the child out to me, but when the child realized she was coming to me, she turned quickly to cling to her Mother and buried her face into her Mother's chest. We all laughed.

Teleel looked at me apologetically.

"Ooooooh, that's okay, sweety! You don't have to come to me! You just stay in your mommy's arms! I bet I do look pretty funny to you!" They chuckled at me.

"You are so pretty! I would never hurt you precious! Do you know I love you? But that's okay you can stay there. I understand."

Precious indeed! A beautiful and very human child with big eyes and a tiny button nose, covered by silky dark hair all over! Even her tiny little ears had fuzz on them! By even the standards of our people, she was a rightfully gorgeous child! I remembered my gift.

"I brought her a gift, may I give it to her?" I asked.

Teluke said "Yes," then he told me to let him see it first. As I automatically turned it over, I gasped that he still didn't trust me! In realizing that he did trust me, he understood this wasn't necessary, so he just glanced at it and gave her the teddy bear.

I explained that I had taken the eyes off because babies like to pick at the eyes, and sometimes they have been known to come off and the child swallow them, so I took them off to protect her. He looked at it curiously.

I had never felt such intense fulfillment of joy. As I bawled and danced I looked at the family. "I am so full! I just don't know what to do with myself! I have never been this happy before! You are so beautiful!"

And they were. Teleel was a gorgeous woman with huge brown eyes and dimples. Her nose was softly rounded at the tip and her lips were full and voluptuous as well. I told her she was a beautiful woman!

"Are all of your women this beautiful?" I was astounded. They said yes, and she flashed a gorgeous "Dolly Parton" smile. I mean she was **BEAUTIFUL!** She was NOT what people expect to see in the popular belief that these are some type of Neanderthal or "ape" race. Believe me! Some of them are equal if not surpassing our make-up! With all of my integrity, I speak the whole truth.

I told them I felt ugly in her presence and they groaned sorrowfully a bit and told me I was nice looking.

She stood there next to Teluke, naked and unashamed. She had all the female bulges and a plump round figure. The hair of her privates was a different texture than the rest of her body hair. Her beautiful breasts hung freely. Her tummy was round and extended slightly, reminding me of my old "Poor Pitiful Pearl" doll I had as a child, with perfectly round child-like shape. Her hips were larger than the rest of her with the usual "saddle-bags" that most women have, clearly distinguishing her female body from Teluke's brawny physique.

It was then that I realized that they were two different kinds of Sasquatch! She was beautifully human looking, while Teluke had a pointed head, no neck, three toes and looked perfectly gorilla!

"You are two different kinds!" I stood there, perplexed.

Teluke looked at Teleel and said "Yes, there are two kinds of our people. Sometimes we take mates with each other."

Not wanting to make too big a deal out of it, I spoke to Teleel freely. "I love you! I have wanted to love you as a girlfriend. I am sorry that I frightened you in the barn that day. I would never hurt you!" I said. "I would never take your baby from you! I never even thought about it! That was his doing!"

"I know that now. I love you too!" She smiled at being able to talk freely with me.

"You don't mind that Teluke is different from you? That his head is pointed and he has three toes?" I asked.

She said no.

I had become so absorbed into talking freely with Teleel that I totally forgot Teluke was even there. Had he listened to our private talk? I shot a glance to him.

"Were you listening to us?" I asked. He affirmed it and I was perturbed as well as highly embarrassed. There was a moment of discomfort for all of us.

"Will I ever see you again?" I asked, changing the subject. Teluke smiled questioningly, uncertain. Raising his eyebrows hopefully, he replied that he didn't know. I could not accept this.

"If we both want it to be, we can make it happen!" I assured them. Teluke nodded, realizing the truth in this.

I squeezed his hand again and told Teleel how much I loved all of them and turned away. They stayed at the fence as I turned back to wave. They waved in return.

At the end of the field I just couldn't contain myself anymore and so I buttoned my cigarettes into my shirt pocket and did four consecutive cartwheels towards the gate and waved good-bye for the last time.

I heard Teluke's thoughts as he gasped in awe and spoke to Teleel, "She rolled away! They sure do strange things with their bodies!"

When I entered the house, Mom was on the phone with the neighbor lady. When she hung up, Mom approached me.

"That was Millie on the phone. She said she was passing the window and looked out and saw you standing at the back fence talking with something. She said she couldn't tell what it was. She said that it looked like a big Polar Bear! Then when she looked again later, there was a black one standing there, also! What was it? What were you talking to?"

I acted puzzled and denied talking with anyone and went on up to my room. I picked white hairs off my flannel sleeve and put them in the cellophane from my cigarette pack. I wanted to label it so it would never get mistaken for something else, but I could not. I had to go on protecting them. I could not take any more risks. If someone found this labeled in my belongings, they would want more details and I'm not good at sidestepping or lying. I just couldn't risk it!

When I went home to my folks, I shared a brief conversation on the Second Attention with my Mother about the Shaman Sasquatch. She fully believed me this time, so I showed her the hair. She asked me where this happened and I could not tell her.

She assured me that I knew her better than that and that she would not let anything happen to them. But I knew how easy things loose control and I told her, "No, Mama. This is where it ends for me. I am going to have to forget all about this myself now. I can't allow myself to think about it anymore or even remember it until they are long gone from my life. I can't risk anyone ever being able to trace them through me. I almost got them killed once and I can't risk it again." She accepted it then.

It took me fifteen years to allow myself to remember it again. My love for them continues to protect them. Both my Mother-in-law and my own Mother have passed away since then. For some unknown reason, Momma absently picked up a pewter Kachina pendant at a garage sale for me simply because she "felt" I might like it. The cellophane sack with his hair sample, I am still looking for.

My Father-in-law, "Pop", remembers the horses not grazing up at the woods suddenly. He recalls the "skunk" that lived around the place. And at last report he recalls having heard movement up in the loft when nothing was found there. I have not spoken to Byron or his sister, who may yet recall some of these events.

My girlfriend, Nan, does remember me telling her about the red eyes we saw in the pasture and how often I went out into the pasture alone, to just stand or sit out there. Most of all, she heard and remembers the thing we could never identify that screamed from the woods several times during the year. What she too recalls sounding like a woman screaming, but yet 'not like a woman', or a large cat screaming, 'yet not like a cat'. Hopefully this book will be a wake-up call to even more memories for them.

My hope in writing this book is also to awaken that part of the readers' consciousness. I know a lot of you also have encountered these beings and shut it out. I am aware of others that also protected these pure beings in this way. I invite you to contact me through the publisher.

I would also once again like to remind the reader that the conversations I have inscribed were basically without "words" because these beings do not have a language per say. In order to share them with you, I had to translate the **knowledge**-transferred via telepathy-into a dialogue for you.

As vibrations begin speeding up, more people will recall they have encountered this non-ordinary reality. Having read this book they may not necessarily choose fear as their reaction, but instead feel familiar with it and begin to relate to these spiritual beings in a more honorable way than we do now. Let there be peace on earth. There is plenty of room for us all.

Blessed Be~~~~~~~White Song Eagle

# Epilogue

## (Full Circle)

"...the time is nigh to see the star

the coming of four ways

a cross of life to rest upon

to ride upon the waves."

SINCE THE RECALL OF THIS fascinating portion of my life, I too needed verification of its actuality. I mean, I can see how unbelievable this is. It happened to me and even I had trouble believing it.

So one night, when I was alone on the 87-acre wetland/farm I have lived on for the past 17 years, I prayed and meditated for answers, clearing my thoughts.

I went in to take a shower and as the water beat down on my head, I prayed again. Having my eyes closed, I suddenly saw a brilliant white light, almost tube like, encase me and my thoughts were sharply focused. I knew the channel was open for communication. I could feel it!

"Teluke! I need you to show me you are **real**! Let me see you, touch you, or do something right now, so I know you are truly **real**! I have to know I'm not crazy! That this REALLY happened!"

**Immediately**, all the power in the house shut down. I'm standing naked in the dark, in total silence except the shower beating on me.

"Wow! That was quick!" I thought. Then a moment later I realized, 'wait a minute. The house is wide open and unlocked. I'm naked in the shower. What if it wasn't Teluke?' Then in my head I heard the screeching music of the movie "Psycho" playing out.

NO! Get a hold of yourself here! It was Teluke. Believe yourself! You can freak yourself out, or accept that he gave you the sign that you needed.

So, I pulled myself together. I shut the water off, groped around in the dark for a towel. Hunted up a lantern and match. I put my robe on, went outside and down into the black cellar. I flipped the main breaker and everything came back on, recreating normalcy for my world.

There had been no storm, no extra power on, no rational purpose for a power failure except that Teluke had directed the energy to overload the breaker himself.

The next day, I was reposing on my air mattress down at the front lake. My silent continual prayer, from the day I reawakened to my Sasquatch interactions, was to reunite with Teluke and Teleel. And since the previous night's event in the shower, my mind never left the subject.

I floated aimlessly in and out of cattails and rushes, out into the center and back as I gazed up at the cerulean sky.

Suddenly, without question, I knew without a doubt that Teluke was coming! I can only surmise that Zanna had confirmed this to me on the Second Attention because the response was immediate, on the conscious level, with absolute knowing!

I hopped off the raft and headed for the beach, receiving the information that it wasn't going to be until tonight, that I didn't need to go to the house just yet.

But, I knew that. I just had a lot to prepare… housework, groceries, all kinds of preparations to make, I'm a woman.

As nighttime rolled around, I waited. I meditated, burned sage, and waited. Eventually, I lay across the bed to take a nap, with the assurance that Zanna would wake me. I was informed that Teluke and Teleel had been moved to another state. They were just learning their way around and Teluke (I found this terribly amusing) had gone exploring a bit too far and had gotten turned around and, well, lost! He didn't want to ask the Star People for help, but it was a long way back.

I woke up and sat in my meditation chair in the front room. The only light was my 30-gallon fish tank by the front door. But you could see well. I had turned my air mattress around, which leaned against the wall, at Zanna's suggestion so that the air cells would not resemble lots of strange eyes looking at my guests from out of the darkness.

Suddenly the floor creaked and I felt their invisible presence in the entranceway. I rose to my feet and a telepathic conversation played itself out in my head without effort. I went over and they sandwiched me between them in a group hug. They were thrilled to see me and we all cried!

Their daughter, who was then 15 years old, did not wish to come down and leave the ship. I led them around the corner and Teluke was astonished to see my painting of Zanna on the dining room wall.

When we passed the mirror he jumped at seeing his reflection, as seen on the Second Attention . I heard him marvel to Teleel about our wonders.

I was flipping back and forth in consciousness and remained in a state of semi-confusion the whole time, trying to be conscious of what was going on, just for my own sanity's sake.

I led them to the kitchen where I fed them raw eggs, carrots, celery, apples and salt. I wanted to load them up with some to take back to the ship, but they refused because they were in good flesh.

They only stayed in the house for about 20 minutes. But they stayed on the property for about 10 days in which time there was constant telepathic communication going on. I had my younger sister over and she heard Teleel's bird like whistle.

He followed me into the cornfield, which oddly enough for the first time, had been partially planted in sweet corn rather than field corn. I took out a wooden bowl and gathered pollen for offering and had a de ja vu, as I once again spoke to someone behind my back "as if he wasn't there" at all.

The house often smelled "skunky" then, and I heard him run through the yard at night with heavy feet, as I would try to catch him in my flashlight beam from the bedroom window. And we enjoyed each other's company.

Even my son, who was then 11 years old, saw someone all white disappear into the hillside by the lake near the barn. He also saw a black arm pass the front door just moments before they banged on the house.

Trying to be conscious of this while it is happening seems to sort of short circuit the connection, just like realizing you are watching something in your peripheral vision that disappears when viewed head on. Just when you become conscious you are looking at red eyes, they are gone. It can be extremely difficult to sort out!

But events continue to happen and maybe with time, hindsight will again reveal the other side of mysteries I continue to live with. I don't claim to know any more than I have stated. These are just some of the pieces. : I realize none of this would hold up in a court for evidence, but this is what I have. It is the kind of evidence that life gives you and it is rarely enough....

For three years after this, I have invited Teluke and his family for Thanksgiving. Each time, as I spend these holidays by myself, they have banged on the walls of my house to let me know they are there.

I am aware of other people in the position of caretaker for these beings, as I am. My point is not to try to convince anyone, because personal experience is the only real thing that will do that.

I have obtained a photograph of a painting done by someone else portraying a female Sasquatch they saw, and it looks like beautiful Teleel, dimples and all. These things are true.

With the exposure to incidents such as these, hopefully people will recognize who and what they encounter and will be able to relate more positively to these spiritual beings.

It is not so unusual for people to run into Sasquatch. It is unusual for people to remember or recognize what they have encountered, as seen in the chapter where we took them swimming in public.

The states of consciousness and states of unconsciousness that I feebly tried to explain of the Sasquatches and myself are further detailed in Eckhart Tolle's book A New Earth. This true story and other Sasquatch encounters apart from my own lies within the boundaries of, and should be addressed from quantum science and not looked upon as science fiction any longer.

Possibly this will serve as a tool of assistance in preparing people when next they may encounter the non-ordinary, which I have no doubt will become much more common in the near future.

We share one world where all creatures were placed in harmony to live in peace and plentitude. Aho!

*Portrait of Teluke in black*

*Teluke sneaking up to the barn at night*

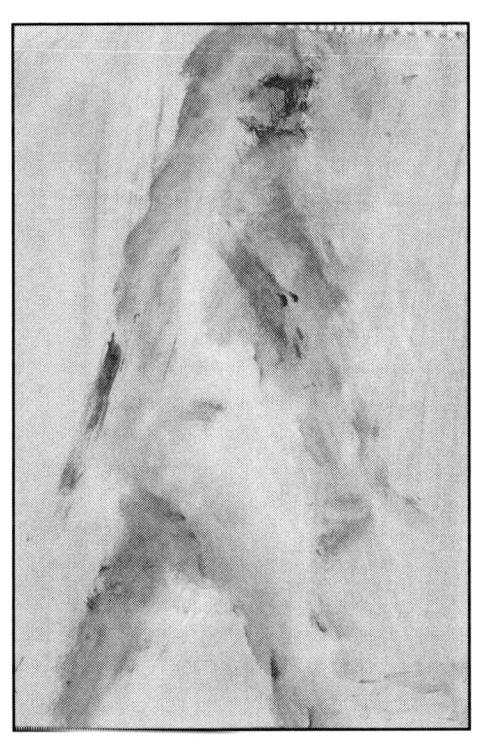

*Teluke taking a whiz behind the barn*

*Teluke at the lake shaking off the water*

*Teluke and Teleel sandwiched the baby between them as they waited for the UFO to come get them.*

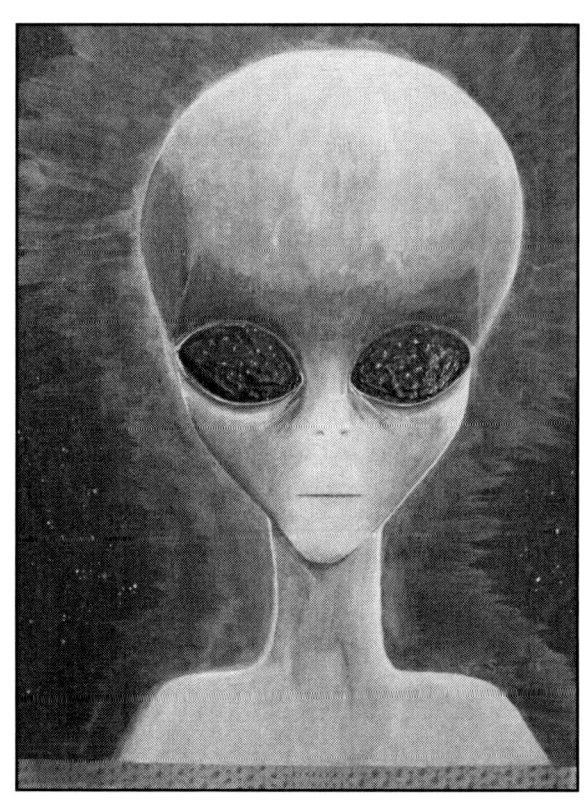

*My portrait of Zanna in blue*

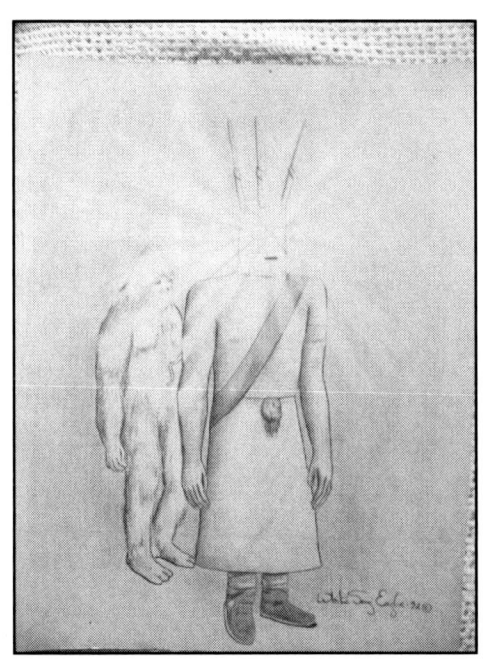

*My drawing of Teluke as a Kachina*

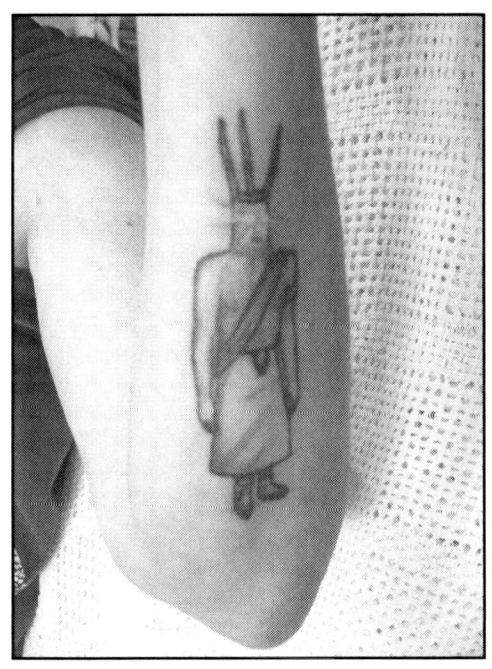

*My tattoo of Teluke as a Kachina*

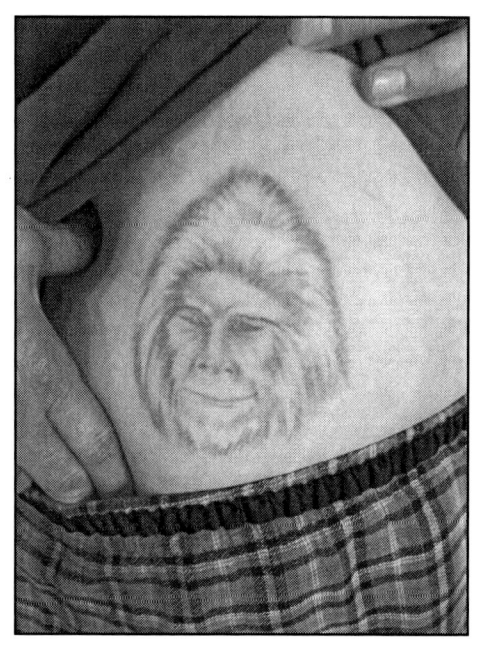

*My tattoo of Teluke from my rendition of him*

*My rendition of Teluke*

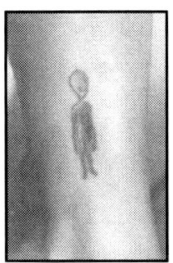

*My tattoo of Zanna from drawing*

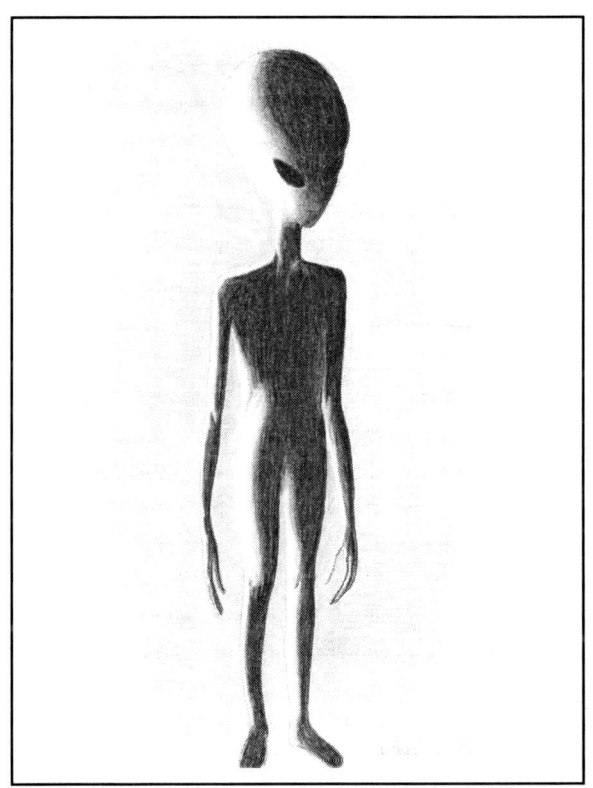

*Channeled drawing of Zanna*

*Me on my palomino riding in the paddock. Teluke's woods is in the background*

*This is the Kachina pendant my mother bought for me*

*This is my show saddle with an unreasonable rope burn in the saddle horn.*

*These are my old horn rimmed glassed Teluke inspected.*

*My little Avon perfume bottle of Roses Roses that Teluke liked.*

*UFO memories*

*Me with a different Big Foot cast taken years later*

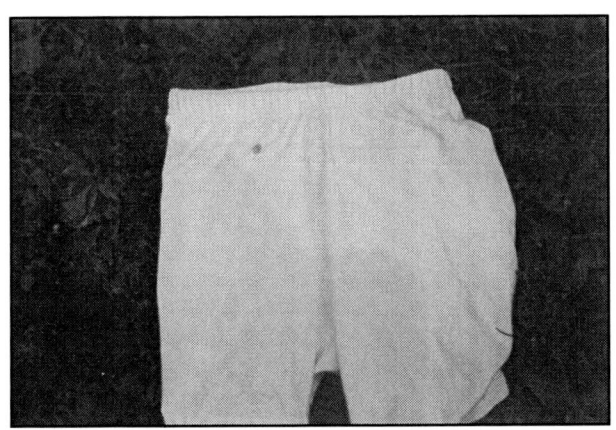

*White shorts with a blood spot at the navel area taken after an abduction on an afternoon walk. Spot is not centered at navel because my shorts where twisted at the waist upon returning. I also had puncture wounds at my fallopian tube area on the front of my body that Debbie Jordan Kauble witnessed.*

# ~ Testimonials ~

To Whom it may concern;

I Donald L. Worley, do hereby state that I have conducted an ongoing investigation and analysis of the claims of the percipient called White Song Eagle. I have found her to be a truthful and objective person. Although the events that this person has experienced are quite unbelievable and bizarre, I state emphatically that she is not mentally deluded, prone to exaggeration. or telling lies. I now have approximately 100 pages of information on her case. What she claims is cobborative with what has happened elsewhere.

I have been a UFO and related ground phenomena investigator-researcher for 25 years. I am now a state section director for the Mutual UFO Network (MUFON). This is the world's largest investigation-research group, based in Texas, USA. In former years I have been with other well known groups such as APRO and CUFOS. In 1976 I presented a paper on my research at the CUFOS International Conference held in Evanston, Illinois. I have investigated over 340 cases of all types.

March 6, 1990
Donald L. Worley

July 5, 1995

To whom it may concern:

I met Whitesong Eagle in June 1988 after she called in to a local radio talk show where I was discussing UFO sightings and abductions. At that time I was an investigator for the Mutual UFO Network and later became State Section Director for central Indiana and Indianapolis, a position I held for six years.

Over the years I have documented and submitted to MUFON a number of sighting and abduction reports from Whitesong. Her experiences began at a very young age and probably continue to the present date, although my records do not cover the last 3-4 years.

One sighting and possible abduction occurred simultaneously with another reported by her neighbor, who was not aware of Whitesong's experiences. I have also talked with a family who lived nearby and they also reported UFO's flying around their property two times in the early morning hours.

Whitesong mentioned some "bigfoot" or Sasquatch sightings but I did not investigate them as I deal mainly with UFO sightings and abductions. However, there may be some correlation.

I believe Whitesong Eagle has had many unusual psychic and UFO related experiences. Many of her experiences have a high similarity to those reported by other abductees. Investigators look for these similarities to help verify stories.

Norma J. Croda

**HEC**

Hoosier
Environmental
Council

June 27, 1995

To whom it may concern:

I have known White Song Eagle for the last six years, since she has been employed at the Hoosier Environmental Council. White Song has been an extremely hard working and dependable employee who believes deeply in HEC and the environmental cause. While she can be opinionated, she also stands out for her honesty and willingness to call things in a straight forward manner. By dependable, I am talking about more than White Song's unflinching willingness to undertake challenging work on HEC's behalf. I mean that she is very conscientious about portraying the issues she is working on in an accurate manner. She studies these issues and cares about what HEC accomplishes on them.

While I ,have not read White Song's book, I can say without hesitation, that its author is a person of the highest calibre for whom I have deep respect.

Sincerely,

Jeffrey Stant
Executive Director

 Recycled Paper

5/31/1995

To whom it may concern:

Ms. White Song Eagle has been with our organization since 1989. I have known her personally since Feb. of 1993. I have worked with her as a fellow employee and as her supervisor since June of 1993. She has also been of great assistance in helping train and working with new employees.

She is always here to do what is assigned, very dependable and a pleasure to work with. I have no reservations with recommending her book. I have never known her to misrepresent anything.

Respectfully

Chester Leatherbury
Canvass Director
Hoosier Environmental Council

325

November 8, 1989

Dear John:

This is meant to serve as a letter of introduction for White Song Eagle of Plainfield, Indiana.

I have known White Song Eagle for 15 months. Because of her interest in my research and her experiences with both the psychic Sasquatch and Starpeople, we met on two occasions and I spent nearly two weeks discussing her encounters. We talked intensely and extensively about these phenomena in her life. I feel strongly that she has had numerous profound contacts with the Bigfoot-people that has scientific value because it gives tremendous insight as to who these elusive nature-beings really are. Since I am convinced that White Song's experiences are genuine and meaningful, I have, if you recall, included a chapter on her in my book entitled: "Teluke: The White Sasquatch".

White Song has written an indepth book about Teluke which I found fascinating. If scientists and lay researchers are to begin to understand the phenomenon behind the phenomena, they need to read and think hard as to the immense implications that books like mine and White Song have written on the subject. Hopefully you will feel the same way I do and perhaps work with her to bring this very important work into the public eye. Therefore, I have referred White Song Eagle to you so that you may review her most unique material.

Sincerely yours,

Jack Lapseritis, B.A., M.S.

"White Song....our bodies are afraid of the visitors—that's natural—but if we let our minds stay terrified as well, we will never be able to set out on the path of greater understanding." Whitley Strieber

– Whitley Strieber is the author of *Communion*

# About the Author

White Song Eagle
Writer, Illustrator and Naturalist

WHITE SONG EAGLE IS AN adopted member of the Eagle Clan of Metosine Meshingomesia Band of Miami Indians of Indiana and is said to walk with one foot in two worlds.

A born naturalist, White Song has a background in animal husbandry. She has been a professional groom and trainer for equines and canines, worked with veterinarians and in Gnotobiotics and is a certified assistant lab technician and thrives in the outdoor environment.

She has served as a nature guide at local parks and has given lectures to school children and civic groups, as well as lobbied for legislation and written articles and environmental columns for local papers and magazines. She also served for 8 years for Indiana's largest environmental group waking people up to healthier choices for the planet.

She is the author of Elevations or AGLA ON Dawning, a book of etheric psalms and wrote a chapter on Big Foot for "The Psychic Sasquatach" by Jack Lapsiritis.

White Song is a practicing massage therapist and Third Degree Reiki Master/Teacher. Her spiritual studies include Energy Medicine techniques, Kinesiology, herbology and natural medicine.

She has enjoyed sky diving, equestrian dressage, has completed a fire walking four times in her bare feet in September 2007 and has experienced the Holy Quickening.

Lightning Source UK Ltd.
Milton Keynes UK
UKOW040739160513

210769UK00001B/28/P